Monographs of the

Rutgers Center of Alcohol Studies

No. 11

Monographs of the Rutgers Center of Alcohol Studies

Under the editorship of MARK KELLER

This monograph series was begun as Monographs of the Yale Center of Alcohol Studies and Numbers 1, 2 and 3 in the series were published at Yale. Beginning with Number 4 the series has been continued as Monographs of the Rutgers Center of Alcohol Studies. The change conforms with the transfer of the Center from Yale to Rutgers University. The works published in this series report the results of original research in any of the scientific disciplines, whether performed at Rutgers or elsewhere.

Firewater Myths

Firewater Myths

North American Indian Drinking and Alcohol Addiction

BY

JOY LELAND

PUBLICATIONS DIVISION
RUTGERS CENTER OF ALCOHOL STUDIES
NEW BRUNSWICK, NEW JERSEY

Copyright © 1976 by
Journal of Studies on Alcohol, Incorporated
New Brunswick, New Jersey

Library of Congress catalog card number: 75-620113
ISBN: 911290-43-5   ISSN: 0080-4983

MANUFACTURED IN THE UNITED STATES OF AMERICA

CONTENTS

List of Tables

List of Charts

Introduction

WITH this comprehensive review and analysis of the literature on Indian drinking Joy Leland sounds a death knell for the popular idea that Indians are constitutionally prone to develop an "inordinate craving for liquor" and to lose control over their behavior when they drink. At the same time, the opposite point of view held by many investigators that alcohol addiction occurs less frequently in this group than in the general population is neither confirmed nor denied by the evidence presented thus far. The lack of agreement as to whether Indian drinking practices are pathological or the expressions of various cultural styles is due to the fact that alcoholism and alcohol addiction are poorly defined concepts. Compounding this confusion is the fact that gathering adequate data among Indian populations is extremely difficult with the result that the interpretation of findings becomes largely a matter of theoretical taste.

Regardless of whether a definition of alcoholism posits the existence of a physiological addiction to or a psychogenic dependence on alcohol, the presence of alcoholism is invariably inferred from its supposed symptoms. The physiological processes of addiction have not been identified and the psychological deficits thought to lead to alcoholism are only identified after the fact. Studies among American Indians have not included independent evaluation of psychological variables to determine whether some are present in populations of heavy drinkers but absent from abstainers.

One popular theory concerning the genesis of alcoholism holds that rapid social change or social disintegration produces psychological stress. This state has been called *anomie* and roughly corresponds to the idea that a form of psychopathology predisposes to alcoholism. Unfortunately, a symptom of anomie such as heavy drinking is used to determine the presence of anomie which is then used to demonstrate the proposition that anomie produces such responses as alcoholism. Direct measures of anomie have not been utilized in studies of Indian populations.

After commenting on this state of affairs in some detail, Leland offers a novel and stimulating suggestion: to study the concept of alcoholism as an *emic* or native category among many others rather than as an *etic* or cross-culturally valid and objectively verifiable one.

I doubt that this approach will determine whether there is such a thing as alcoholism or whether sizable numbers of Indians are, in fact, alcoholics. The essentially ethnographic methods of ethnoscience predispose toward results of a cultural nature. It is questionable whether social scientists should turn their backs on hypotheses utilizing physiological explanations or on quantitative and comparative research in general. Indeed, recent work by Fenna and associates[1] suggests that Indians and Orientals may metabolize alcohol more slowly than Anglos. While I do not believe these differences are sufficient to account for different drinking styles, I am convinced that categorical denial of physiologically based differences between various populations of the world should not be allowed to direct interest away from this potentially significant area of investigation. Nevertheless, following Leland's suggestion that social scientists stop using the term alcoholism and pay more attention to cultural usages and definitions generally will enable us to look at the social effects which result from the labeling of Indian behaviors as pathological by the dominant society.

Our ideas concerning the nature of the Indian, the North American landscape, alcohol, and even ourselves as a people have changed radically since colonial times. To the Puritan settlers the wild nature of the New World was a wilderness to be conquered and tamed. The Indian, a man of nature, was also wild and to be domesticated. He was, in fact, a living example of what the civilized Christian must not be but is forever tempted to become by Satan himself. Alcohol was the means by which a Christian was tempted and ultimately destroyed. The Indian, conveniently perhaps, drank to excess and so confirmed the colonists' world view.

During the 19th century the frontiers were closed, the wilderness disappeared and Indians were safely confined to reservations. No longer a barrier to westward expansion, the Indian became the recipient of Christian charity. As the nation became industrialized, Americans began to mourn the loss of untrammeled nature and the Indian became the pitiable remnant of a noble race which once had

[1] FENNA, D., MIX, L., SHAEFER, D, and GILBERT, J. A. L. Ethanol metabolism in various racial groups. Canad. med. Ass. J. 105: 472-475, 1971.

lived in harmony with that nature. Alcohol was still a destructive substance and the drinker still a moral degenerate but to many the alcoholic was more an unfortunate product of industrialization than a willful and evil pervert. Church and welfare groups worked among the urban immigrants and, during Grant's presidency, missionaries were put in charge of Indian reservations.

The 20th century has witnessed the ascendance of science and with it the growth of the medical profession. Many areas once the province of the churchmen are now handled by medical people. Social deviants are rehabilitated by psychologists and the insane are treated by medical personnel. Even childbirth has been taken from the midwife in the home and treated as if it were a disease, in a hospital, controlled by medical doctors, with the mother supine, bound and drugged like a patient in surgery. In like manner the deviant drinker is increasingly being thought of as sick rather than degenerate. He is detoxicated in hospital wards, treated with drugs, and given therapy by psychologists and psychiatrists. There is no doubt that many of these developments have had beneficial effects when viewed medically. The social effects of the adoption of what has been called the medical model have not been comprehensively assessed.

It is my impression that the American Indian is seriously affected by a growing tendency to approach his social, economic and personal problems exclusively from the scientific point of view. Indian societies are subordinate to the national society. Personal success is often attained by accepting dominant-society definitions and behavioral modes. All too frequently this involves the acceptance of a negative image of the self. Without implying that the image of the Indian as a moral inferior is preferable to the image of the Indian as a sick alcoholic, a member of a sick, disintegrated society, it is important to point out that it is probably more difficult to reject a scientific judgment pronounced by an objective and disinterested professional than one espoused by a recent conqueror who is also a member of a strange proselytizing religion.

Though it is the right of the Indian as an American citizen and of the various tribes as parties to treaties with the Federal Government to receive such services, opportunities and benefits as are provided other citizens, in practice funding is often provided only after a need has been established. The National Institute of Mental Health and recently the National Institute on Alcohol Abuse and Alcoholism, among many other agencies, have been most active in encouraging research and treatment programs in Indian communities. In order to qualify for these funds, however, some problem such as drinking must be demonstrated. Increasingly the Indian must define himself as sick in order to get Federal monies. The morally degenerate may save themselves by embracing Christianity, but the sick are saved by accepting treatment, a far more passive stance indeed.

The underdevelopment of reservation economies has often been remarked. Less frequently commented upon is the fact that these economies are heavily oriented to the service industries. Income on the vast Navaho Reservation, for instance, is primarily from Federal and tribal expenditures. Moreover, virtually all Federal money and a significant proportion of the tribal budget are devoted to human services. The Office of Navaho Economic Opportunity spent $400,000 in 1971 for alcoholism programs in a reservation population of approximately 130,000 people. It appears that the path to occupational and social advancement for Indians lies in the professions dealing with human services.[2]

One of the consequences of this form of economic development, it seems to me, is a polarization of the Indian population. The educated Indian who prefers to live on the reservation must prepare himself for these "helping" occupations. To be successful he must internalize and accept the health and welfare goals and concepts of the agency where he works. He is one of the very few on his reservation who is employed and he is helping his people by ministering to them. Ultimately, the better educated and employed Indians come to see their unemployed fellows, who comprise some 60% of most reservation labor forces, as sick or in some way debilitated.

Clearly, neither the Federal Government nor the professionals involved in these programs or in research intend that the Indian see himself as sick. On the contrary, the aim has been to bring modern services to rural Indian populations. Nevertheless, so long as alcoholism, suicide, homicide and the like are defined as symptoms of anomie or social pathology and so long as the prevalence of these occurrences is used to justify many of the treatment and research programs, I do not see how either the professional or the Indian can avoid viewing reservation communities and the individuals within them as, in some sense, sick.

[2] Kunitz, S. J. Personal communication.

Such a self-image is, of course, realistic if disease in fact is present. But alcoholism and other supposed symptoms of social pathology have neither been shown invariably to manifest individual pathology nor even to represent social pathologies present only in sick societies. They may, of course, ultimately be shown to be just that, and well controlled research should continue both among Indians and in the society at large. In the meantime, however, Leland's suggestion that social scientists forego the use of the term alcoholism and turn their attention to questions concerning the social functions of labeling behaviors as deviant and the changing notions of deviance in our own as well as other societies is a most welcome one. More awareness in these areas may indeed provide a more constructive and less pejorative climate within which continuing research on alcohol use may proceed.

JERROLD E. LEVY

Department of Anthropology
University of Arizona

1

The Old Myth and the New

THE FIREWATER MYTH probably deserves the endurance record for unfounded folklore about American Indians. According to this myth, Indians are constitutionally prone to develop an inordinate craving for liquor and to lose control over their behavior when they drink.

The term "firewater" does not appear in North American literature until the 19th century.[1] However, the myth which eventually employed the term developed much earlier. For example, about the end of the 17th century, Abbé Belmont (9, *p. 49*) described the Ottawa as "addicted"[2] and "passionately attached" to brandy and noted with horror Bacchanalian excesses which occurred when they drank. Similar behavior was recorded among many other Indian groups.[3] According to Dailey (28, *p. 22*), "In the absence of the anthropological concept of culture, the first Europeans naturally interpreted the Indians' response to alcohol as a constitutional or racial difference. Undoubtedly, this is the origin of the 'firewater theory' of Indian alcoholism."

The notion that Indians are constitutionally unable to handle liquor continued into the 19th century, as the following statement by Schoolcraft (170, *p. 192*) illustrates: "It is strange how all the Indian nations, and almost every person among them, male and fe-

---

[1]Oxford English Dictionary, 1961 ed.

[2]The application of the term "addiction" to forms of heavy drinking is 20th-century usage, according to Marconi (126, *p. 230*), which has not been incorporated into the firewater myth. However, the "craving" depicted in the myth may be interpreted as implying "addiction" in the modern sense. If Marconi is correct in dating this term, it would be interesting to see what word Belmont used in the original French which has been translated as "addicted" in the English version (9, *p. 49*). Unfortunately the document in French is not readily available.

[3]For example, see the documentation in Belmont (9); Bourke (11); Clark (24); Dailey (29); Delanglez (32, *pp. 69–129*); Frederickson (51); Henderson (64, *p. 1*); Horton (71, *pp. 298–300*); Howay (72); MacAndrew and Edgerton (121); Salone (167); Vachon (203); Winkler (216).

male, are infatuated with the love of strong drink. They know no bounds to their desire, while they can swallow it down, and then indeed the greatest man among them scarcely deserves the name of brute."

Early in this century, the judge in a Nevada Supreme Court case remarked:[4] "Counsel for the defendants have dwelt in their briefs upon the point that the defendants were Indians, and that, as a matter of general knowledge, intoxicating liquor more readily destroys the mental faculties of the Indian than it does those of the White man."

Today, the firewater myth still persists. It is still popularly believed that some hereditary peculiarity makes it impossible for Indians to drink without disastrous consequences. Some Indians share this view. For example, a prominent female Indian activist recently declared: "No Indian should have liquor. Because of the way our bodies absorb sugar it goes straight to our brains. Liquor has the same effect on Indians that drugs have on whites." (223, p. 41).

The statements quoted above set forth the main allegations of the firewater myth: genetic characteristics peculiar to Indians cause them to respond to alcohol by exhibiting (1) exceptional changes for the worse in comportment and (2) an inordinate craving for the drug.

That the belief in this myth is not confined to non-Indians has been noted by numerous authors.[5] Evidently many Indians either believe the myth's stereotypes or at least pretend to believe them for strategic reasons.

The notion that there is a genetic basis for the Indians' alleged reaction to liquor has been declared untenable in view of the racial hybridization of those who are legally or self-defined as Indians (184, pp. 61, 64; 36, p. 74). In addition, it is ironic that among peoples who have been grouped together under the anthropometric racial classification "Mongoloid," some are noted for a low rate of alcohol addiction and for markedly decorous behavior when drinking,[6] while others, including the American Indians, have the opposite reputation.

[4]*State v. Johnny*; in: Douglass and Noel (35, *pp. 225*).

[5]Boyer (14, *p. 218*); Chance (21, *p. 68*); Clairmont (22, *p. 8*; 23, *p. 66*); Dailey (28, *p. 22*); Hamer (58, *p. 298*); Henderson (65, *p. 67*); Kaplan and Johnson (89, *p. 217*); Koolage (99, *p. 101*); Lemert (108, *pp. 102-103*); Swett (241, *pp. 8, 24*).

[6]For example, the American Chinese: Barnett (8); Field (49, *p. 70*) quoting Snyder (177); Wang (207, *p. 260*); Wilkinson (215, *p. 219*). And the Japanese: Lemert (107, *p. 379*); Moore (137); Ushijima (200).

A number of experts who have reviewed the evidence concluded that it does not support a genetic basis for the firewater myth. For example, Dailey (28, *p. 26*) states, "The Indian is not constitutionally prone to the effects of alcohol," and Dozier (36, *p. 74*) writes, "Recognition of the Indian as primarily a social entity rather than a biological unit is important in dispelling the notion, still held by many people, that Indian drinking is racially connected." Mindell (237, *p. 8*) dismisses as "myth" the notion that Indians "have a different tolerance to alcohol than non-Indians. . . . There is no reason to believe this is true." The Indian Health Service Task Force on Alcoholism (75, *p. 3*) concludes: "No valid evidence is available that Indians differ in any way from others in their physiological or constitutional response to alcohol." Diethelm (34, *p. 13*) says:

"There is no indication from this direct observation that the American Indian is more susceptible to alcohol than the other inhabitants of the United States. The behavior when intoxicated is an accepted uncontrolled behavior and essentially the same as found in other groups in our population, especially in late adolescents. There is no indication that it relates to special constitutional factors. Differences between the reactions of American Indians and other inhabitants of this country seem to depend on sociologic and not racial factors."

Brody (16, *p. 35*) concludes:

"There is no evidence within the literature on alcohol to date to confirm that the Indians, as a race, are less able to tolerate the effects of alcohol . . . I found no basis for the view that Indians [on Skid Row in Ottawa] have as a matter of chemistry constitutionally less resistance to alcohol. It may seem laborious to continue emphasizing this lack of evidence, but the insistence with which non-Indians hold the belief is disturbing since it provides in all social contexts . . . a rationale for discriminatory practices."

However, it is only fair to point out that the foregoing opinions are based on negative evidence. Because of the lack of theoretical grounds for any expectation that genetic characteristics might make Indians constitutionally vulnerable to the effects of alcohol, experiments to test this hypothesis had not been conducted at the time these statements were made.

Recent evidence suggests that the question deserves further study. In a small group (64 subjects), Indians and Eskimos were found to metabolize alcohol at a significantly slower rate than Whites. The difference was not correlated with either the diet or the customary alcohol intake of the subjects, "leaving genetic factors as the indicated cause" (45, p. 472).

Nevertheless, even if these findings are borne out by further research, the mechanism by which slower metabolism could result in inordinate craving for alcohol or unusually disorderly drunken comportment among Indians (the other two main themes of the firewater myth) is not obvious.

On the basis of both historical and modern accounts, MacAndrew and Edgerton (121) have impressively demonstrated that alcohol does not inevitably cause Indians to become drunk and disorderly, or to crave more. This is perhaps the best evidence to date that Indians do not have genetic peculiarities which condition their responses to alcohol. If members of many tribes, today and in the past, could drink without exhibiting the behavior alleged by the firewater myth, then Indian responses to alcohol could not be genetically determined.

However, MacAndrew and Edgerton's evidence still leaves open the possibility that, for nongenetic reasons, Indians do indeed exhibit (more markedly than other folk) the behavior attributed to them by the myth, which of course would not be precluded even if the genetic theme of the firewater myth were definitely discredited.

The allegation that disruptive behavior in association with alcohol is more frequent and more severe among Indians than in the general population is made by most observers, Indian as well as non-Indian, of current Indian drinking. Some of the evidence on this point will be summarized later.

The drunken comportment of Indians, however, is not the main focus here. Instead, the principal theme will be the firewater-myth doctrine that alcohol creates an inordinate craving for liquor among Indians. Such behavior suggests the familiar Alcoholics Anonymous description of the alcohol addict—"one drink away from a drunk." Thus, the "craving" motif can be, and seems to be, popularly interpreted as claiming that Indians who drink are doomed to become alcohol addicts.

This stereotype seems even more damaging to Indians than the "drunk and disorderly" image. Perhaps for this reason, many observers of Indian drinking have taken particular pains to refute this portion of the myth. A number of authors have pointed out that they have seen no evidence of unusual "craving" for alcohol in the Indian groups they studied. In fact, many authorities have gone one step further, declaring that, despite the acknowledged prevalence of problem drinking among North American Indians, alcohol addiction is actually rare in the Indian groups they have studied.

The main objective here is to examine the scattered literature on American Indian drinking to see whether the evidence therein justifies the allegation that alcohol addiction occurs less frequently in this group than in the general population. Do all observers agree that alcohol addiction is rare in the Indian groups on which they report? Do they agree that a common set of symptoms of alcohol addiction is rare in the groups in question? Are such conclusions warranted by the evidence on which they are based?

If these questions can be answered affirmatively, we could say that the firewater myth's "craving" motif has not only been refuted—e.g., by MacAndrew and Edgerton (121)—but has also been turned upside down.

In view of the popular conviction that Indians are more prone to alcohol addiction than others, it would be ironic, indeed, if we were to find not only that the affliction occurs no more frequently in this group than in others but, actually, less frequently.

To emphasize this irony, I will preempt the name of the entire myth and refer to this proposition as the "reverse-firewater hypothesis." However, it should be emphasized that reversal of the "craving" motif, alone, provides only a partial mirror image of the firewater myth, since it has no bearing on the "drunken comportment" motif. Even if alcohol addiction were proved to be rare in this group, that would not preclude the possibility that Indians do indeed become extraordinarily drunk and disorderly when they drink, as the "drunken comportment" motif suggests, or that this response may be genetically influenced. On the other hand, it would suggest that if the genetic make-up of Indians is peculiar in ways that affect their response to alcohol, in the case of "craving" it serves somehow to protect them from alcohol addiction, contrary to the firewater myth.

The reverse-firewater hypothesis appears most often in the writings of anthropologists, but it shows up in statements by members of other disciplines and professions as well. Quoted below are the passages which I interpret as advocating that alcohol addiction is rare among the American Indian groups to which the statements refer. Unless otherwise indicated, the statements are made by anthropologists.

Berreman (10, *p. 511*) says of an Aleut group: "In spite of the continued, heavy and extended drinking by some villagers, and frequent indulgence by nearly all, there have been no observed or reported cases of true alcoholism, of compulsive or addictive drinking, in Nikolski."

Chance (21, *p. 69*) states categorically that "there is no . . . alcoholism" among the Eskimo groups on which he reports.

Dailey (28, *p. 26*) says that among North American Indians "drinking is periodic and explosive, but non-addictive."

Devereux (33, *p. 208*) remarks on the rarity of "systematic excessive use of alcohol by even a small fraction of the [Mohave] population."

Dozier (36, *p. 72*) says, "observation of Indian drinking patterns indicates that . . . individual addicted drinkers are perhaps less common among Indians than among other groups," although he disclaims any attempt "to isolate the medically diagnosed alcoholic from the habitual excessive drinker whose drinking may not have progressed to the point of addiction."

Hamer (58, *p. 294*) reports that among the "Whitehorse" Potawatomi, "There are only two individuals who might be classed as compulsive drinkers; the vast majority seem capable of getting along without liquor."

Heath (63, *p. 129*) states that about 15% of the Navaho population on which he reports are "heavy drinkers" but, "Even among these . . . there is no instance of individual dependence on alcohol."

Discussing drinking among Whites and natives in a small Alaska town, the Honigmanns (68, *p. 614*) say, "the one confirmed alcoholic" is White. John Honigmann[7] confirms that it was his impression that alcohol addiction was rare in this Kaska Indian group at the time of the study.

Lemert reported that alcohol addiction was absent in three Salish tribes (108, *p. 106*). Among the Northwest Coast Indians in general, he notes (107, *p. 362*), "Although excessive, sustained drunkenness occurs in coastal Indians, it is symptomatic rather than compulsive or addictive in nature."

Rohner and Rohner (165, *p. 48*) say, "The incidence of alcoholism among the Kwakiutl is reported to be very low. We know of no Kwakiutl, in fact, who can be correctly diagnosed as an alcoholic."

In addition to the anthropologists cited above, members of several

[7]Honigmann, J. J. Personal communication, 21 June 1971.

other disciplines and professions have suggested that alcohol addiction rarely occurs among the Indian groups they discuss.

Littman, a social worker, although he expresses distrust of generalizations about "Indians" as a group, notes (117, *p. 1778*) that "much of American Indian alcoholism appears to coincide" with that of Finnish lumbermen, who, he says, "do not become addicted to alcohol."

McKinley (123, *p. 32*), assistant director of Indian education at Arizona State University, says, "as bad as alcoholism may be on the Indian Reservations . . . it has not as yet become really acute." Recently, two pioneers in the field of Indian alcoholism, Dr. Wayne S. Wellman, who has completed a study and developed a film on alcoholism for the Navaho Tribe, and V. W. Werner, executive director of the S.I.A.C. [Southwest Indian Alcoholism Council] and formerly educational director of the New Mexico Commission on Alcoholism, said that "there are very few 'true' or addictive Indian alcoholics at the present time."

Werner (209, *p. 1*), one of the "pioneers" quoted above, has said that among Indians, "Today we have a high degree of problem drinking, but alcoholism per se is not as large at the present time as it is among other peoples."

Concerning an isolated Indian community notorious for its high alcohol consumption, a B.I.A. (Bureau of Indian Affairs) community planner is quoted (152, *p. 5*) as saying, "there are probably no alcoholics in the tribe."

Sanchez (168, *p. 3*), a B.I.A. community living guidance specialist, generalizing about Indians as a group, says, "In the experience I have had as a social worker with Indians, I have tended to come to the conclusion that the Indian does not do the extreme kind of drinking which we tend to associate with the word 'alcoholism.' He drinks when he has money. It is a social affair and tends to be of the 'binge' type but there are few indications that he has become addicted to the drinking."

Two physicians and a social worker (187, *p. 1*) state that among their Navaho patients, "65 percent develop a habituation to alcohol and must drink into the week in an effort to avoid increasingly severe hangovers. In the total group, however, only two could be characterized as clinical alcoholics with outright dependency needs."

When he was in charge of the Indian Health Service, physician

Caruth J. Wagner is said to have questioned that there was much true alcoholism on the reservation (40).

Another physician (52, *p. 196*) has said, "the Apaches do not become addicted or continuously intoxicated over relatively long periods of time," although he expressed the opinion that their binge drinking qualifies as a form of "alcoholism."

The opinions quoted above were expressed casually, as incidental to the primary focus of the works in which they appear. None of these authors professed to have systematically investigated the incidence of alcohol addiction in the groups they discussed. Some of the quotations are from secondary sources; a few appear in speeches made to laymen and might have been expressed differently if they had been addressed to an audience of professionals.

Nevertheless, taken together, these statements indicate that a number of experienced observers in several fields share the opinion that alcohol addiction may be absent or rare in the Indian groups they report upon. These groups include the nation's largest tribe, the Navaho, and a wide variety of geographically separate peoples from diverse aboriginal cultures.

The reverse-firewater hypothesis does not merely challenge the notion that Indians are more prone to alcohol addiction than dominant-society members; it offers a counterproposal that Indians may be even less susceptible to this affliction.

Thurber's "Bear Who Let It Alone" became more troublesome as a teetotaler than he had been as a drunkard. The moral of the fable was, "You might as well fall flat on your face as lean over too far backward" (188, *p. 253*). Perhaps it is time for students of Indian drinking to heed this warning.

Evidence has been accumulating for over 3 centuries that Indian drinking lends itself to myth-making and stereotyping. Thus, reporting on this subject requires unusual care. As statements accumulate in the literature suggesting that alcohol addiction is rare in this or that Indian group, it becomes increasingly important to examine critically the basis for this conclusion. The practical implications are great. To mention only one, the Office of Economic Opportunity in 1970–71 funded "alcoholism" treatment programs affecting over 30 tribes (210). The composite approaches to problem drinking used by most of these programs usually include components which presuppose the presence of alcohol addiction, such as Alcoholics Anonymous methods or the administration of disulfiram (a drug which causes disagreeable symptoms if alcohol is drunk). But if there is little or no alcohol addiction, then the wrong problem is being attacked and inappropriate methods applied. The present study will examine the evidence on the nature of the problem by comparing the reported drinking-related behaviors of North American Indians with the classical behavior and symptoms presumed to be indicative of alcoholism or alcohol addiction.

2

Definitions of Alcoholism

A PRINCIPAL OBSTACLE to evaluation of the evidence relating to the hypothesis that alcohol addiction is rare in the Indian groups concerning whom this phenomenon has been reported, or in any group, for that matter, is lack of agreement on the meaning of terms. The alcohol literature abounds with statements that no definition of "alcoholism" is generally accepted. The variation in definitions reflects fundamental disagreement about the nature of "alcohol addiction," the differing theoretical orientation and technical terminology of the participating disciplines, jurisdictional disputes, policy controversies (e.g., revolving around the disease concept of alcoholism), semantic problems, and, above all, the mystery of the etiology of this phenomenon.

Confusion is further compounded by the use of the term "alcoholism," sometimes as a synonym for "alcohol addiction" (as illustrated in some of the statements already quoted), sometimes as a cover term for both addicted and nonaddicted habitual excessive drinking, and with a variety of other meanings as well. Even more troublesome, the term "alcoholism" is often used without definition.

Keller (96, *p. 19*) warned that, although discriminating usage would make a distinction between alcoholism and alcohol addiction, "the term alcoholism must be understood as probably including alcohol addiction except when the two are expressly distinguished. Determining the meaning of alcoholism in the literature at present may require close attention to context."

Definitions of "alcoholism" can be divided into the following categories: *(1)* definitions emphasizing causes, *(2)* definitions emphasizing effects, and *(3)* definitions combining both causes and effects. The causes and effects contained in these definitions may be further divided into four subcategories: *(a)* pharmacological, *(b)* physiopathological or other physical, *(c)* psychological and psychiatric, *(d)* social and cultural. Within these subcategories a bewildering array of further subdivisions of categories is offered in the definitions.

I shall not attempt to quote or to cite examples of definitions which

10

I would include in each of these categories. Such a summary would require considerable space, and examples of each are easily identified in several extensive compilations of definitions already available.[1]

The "causes" included in the etiologically oriented definitions remain hypotheses. It is generally agreed that the causes of alcoholism are thus far unknown.[2]

A "cause" should be present before the effect appears. So far, no characteristics in any of the subcategories listed above have been definitely established as antecedents of alcohol addiction. The postulated "causes" may be the result of prolonged heavy intake of alcohol. Failure to take this possibility into account by proponents of various etiologies is frequently criticized in the alcohol literature.[3]

Speculation about the causes of problem drinking has been a major preoccupation of the literature on Indian alcohol use. A bewildered journalist (195, *p. 1*), after a brief look at some of the pertinent works, remarked, "When it comes to explaining why Indians drink so much there are research findings to support or refute practically any theory." Prominent theories postulate the following as causes of excessive drinking among Indians: acculturation stress, anomie, the pursuit of ecstasy, and social structure. Many other causes have been proposed; a selection of these will be listed below.[4]

In this study I shall not attempt to deal with the problem of the etiology of Indian alcoholism, whether conceived of as an addiction or not. A review and evaluation of current theories would require extensive separate treatment. Furthermore, the question of why Indians drink as they do may seem premature after a review of the literature has highlighted how little is known about how they drink —the behavior for which a cause is sought.

More important, the question of etiology seems irrelevant to the focus here since, according to King (98, *p. 332*), "Cause is not an intrinsic part of diagnosis."

If the cause is not an intrinsic part of diagnosis, it is difficult to

[1]For example, Bowman and Jellinek (12); Jellinek (84); Keller (91); Keller and McCormick (95); Keller and Seeley (96). Marconi reviewed the history of the development of the concept "alcohol addiction" (126).

[2]Keller (90, *p. 2*; 91, *p. 311*); Smith (176, *p. 5*); Syme (186, *p. 301*); Ullman (196, *p. 49*); Wilkins and Wesson (214, *p. 72*).

[3]For example, Cooperative Commission (26, *p. 46*); Lester (109, *p. 431*); Pittman and Snyder (156, *pp. 390, 391*); Robins et al. (163, *p. 395*) U.S. National Center for Prevention and Control of Alcoholism (199, *p. 24*).

[4]See Ch. 4, footnote 47.

understand the complaint of Levy and Kunitz (113, *p. 220*) that the presence of alcoholism must be "invariably determined by its supposed manifestations" because no directly observable causes have been discovered. They thus imply that causes would be preferable to "manifestations" as bases for diagnosis. But as King (98, *p. 331*) points out, "We must agree with David Hume who emphasized that we never *observe* a cause. No more do we observe a diagnosis; we infer it from the data at hand. The data constitute the 'signs,' while the diagnosis, the entity signified, is arrived at by an inferential leap from these observed signs."

It appears, then, that whether we are dealing with causes or effects, diagnosis must be inferred from manifestations. Nevertheless, since the causes of alcohol addiction are unknown, it follows that an evaluation of the hypothesis that alcohol addiction is rare in certain Indian groups must necessarily be based on a definition of "alcoholism" which deals with manifestations of effects. Among these, the most widely accepted (172, *p. 352*) is the one adopted by the Alcoholism Subcommittee of the World Health Organization's Expert Committee on Mental Health (220, *p. 16*):

"Alcoholics are those excessive drinkers whose dependence upon alcohol has attained such a degree that it shows a noticeable mental disturbance or an interference with their bodily and mental health, their interpersonal relations, and their smooth social and economic functioning; or who show the prodromal signs of such developments. They therefore require treatment."

"Excessive drinkers," of which the alcoholics described above are considered a sub-group by the WHO Subcommittee, are those whose drinking

"in its extent goes beyond the traditional and customary 'dietary' use, or the ordinary compliance with the social drinking customs of the whole community concerned" *(p. 15)*.

The Subcommittee also stated that the category it described as "alcoholics" can be divided into two groups: alcohol addicts and habitual symptomatic excessive drinkers. As an elaboration of the distinction between these two groups the Subcommittee provided, as an "Annex" (220, *pp. 26–39*), E. M. Jellinek's famous "Phases of Alcohol Addiction," later republished with an important modification in the Quarterly Journal of Studies on Alcohol (81).[5] A biometrician and educator who was one of the world's leading alcohol scholars

[5]This will be the source cited herein.

(26, *p. 41*) until his death in 1963, Jellinek remains the most widely quoted authority in the field. In his "Phases of Alcohol Addiction," Jellinek described a constellation of symptoms thereof and explained how to distinguish between addictive alcoholics and habitual symptomatic excessive drinkers, a distinction which I will discuss later. For brevity, he suggested substituting the term "nonaddictive alcoholics" for the latter category, a practice which I will follow.

For anthropologists, perhaps the most striking feature of the World Health Organization definition is its acknowledgment of the relativity of "excessive" drinking. However, the definition has been declared deficient and difficult to apply principally because it is relativistic. Thus Seeley (172, *p. 353*) says: "Applied in rigor, it lumps together a member of a teetotaling 'community concerned' who takes one drink, and the highest-intake messmate in a regularly free-drinking mess. The probability of finding biological identities or similarities in such classification seems small." In fact, the probability of finding identities of any kind in such a population seems small.

The necessity of relying on a definition based on manifestations of effects (e.g., the Jellinek symptoms) to determine the presence of alcohol addiction presents serious problems for cross-cultural research, as pinpointed by Levy and Kunitz (113, *pp. 220–221*):

"First, all of the manifestations of alcoholism have come to our attention through experience with heavy drinkers in our own and other Western societies. There is no guarantee that a similar association will prevail in another culture. Moreover, as the diagnosis must be made on the basis of manifestations, there is no method readily available for testing the validity of the association in other cultures. Secondly, all of the manifestations are, to a greater or lesser degree, culturally defined and determined, especially those used as indicators in most epidemiological investigations. The economic ill effects of drinking are defined and measured by Western standards as are the social effects of broken homes, overt aggression, etc. In an Indian society where divorce was common in aboriginal times, where economic opportunities are limited for drinkers and nondrinkers alike and where arrests are made for breaches of White rather than aboriginal norms and laws, it is difficult to determine whether these behaviors are caused by drinking, are themselves causes of drinking, or are fortuitously associated due to the fact that all these behaviors occur frequently in many Indian communities.

"Most investigators would agree that the more physiologically based indicators like Laënnec's cirrhosis or the withdrawal syndrome are less culture bound than are the behavioral manifestations. Yet it is just such data which have been lacking in virtually all studies of Indian drinking to date. It is not surprising then to find many investigators inferring the presence or absence of alcoholism in Indian societies in light of preconceived notions about the nature of Indians themselves as well as about the causes and effects of alcoholism."

Few observers of Indian drinking explicitly state which of the many definitions has served as the criterion for their opinion about the occurrence of alcohol addiction in the Indian groups they report upon. They do provide us with some clues, however. Their opinions are often accompanied by reports that specific behaviors or effects of drinking (manifestations) do or do not occur in the group concerned.[6] I interpret these statements as indicating that the author believes such elements are symptomatic of alcohol addiction and that he bases his opinion about the occurrence of alcohol addiction on the incidence of these elements which he reports.

The regularity with which several of these symptoms occur in the descriptions suggests that a rather uniform folk category of "alcohol addiction" is shared by many observers, despite the confusion present in the formal definitions. This folk category in turn may reflect a popular American belief that most if not all alcoholics conform to a Skid Row stereotype (134, *p. 19;* 26, *p. 113*). A few of the proponents of the reverse-firewater hypothesis appear to base their opinions primarily upon the apparent absence of alleged Skid Row behavior in the Indian group on which they report. For example, Lemert (107, *p. 362*) says: "The familiar picture of the White chronic alcoholic of the addictive type, who drinks to excess for many years, loses jobs, is divorced or separated from his family, spends time off and on in hospitals and jails, and finally ends on Skid Row 'mooching' drinks and begging money, seems to be absent among the Coastal Indians."

Lemert is to be commended for providing this relatively explicit description of the behavior he believes to be absent among the Northwest Coast Indians. However, such behavior actually is absent in most people who are labeled alcohol addicts by the dominant society (157, *p. 38;* 199, *p. 7*), including the majority of Skid Row inhabitants.[7] Therefore, the fact that members of an Indian group

---

[6]For example, see the statements quoted in the discussion in Chapter 4 of Symptom 16A, solitary drinking.

[7]E.g., Cooperative Commission (26, *p. 113*); Mendelson (134, *p. 17*) and Wallace (205, *p. 132*).

do not meet the Skid Row criteria is insufficiant justification for the conclusion that alcohol addiction is rare among them.

I do not claim that Skid Row derelicts or any other particular model have been the standard to which most observers have compared drinking behavior in various Indian groups as a basis for their opinions on the occurrence of alcohol addiction among them. I have not attempted to delineate systematically the folk category of alcohol addiction represented in this literature. Most observers have not provided us with their own model of alcohol addiction. Among those who have been relatively explicit on this point the criteria vary greatly.

3

Method

SEVERAL OBSERVERS have expressed the opinion that alcohol addiction is rare in the North American Indian groups they have studied. I shall examine the evidence in the literature on alcohol use covering these and a number of other Indian groups in an effort to determine whether it supports or refutes this reverse-firewater hypothesis.

Generalizations about the occurrence of alcohol addiction in these groups should be based on a standard set of criteria. In the absence of such a framework in the literature consulted, I use the Jellinek symptoms of alcohol addiction (81) mentioned in the preceding chapter.

The choice of this instrument seems justifiable on a number of grounds. For one thing, the author enjoys the highest respect of students of alcohol use.[1] More important, Jellinek's is one of the few works aimed directly at the identification of addictive drinking and its differentiation from nonaddictive drinking. Some 18 years ago Jackson (77, *p. 248*) remarked, "Jellinek has published the only detailed descriptions of alcoholic drinking attitudes and behaviors."

Subsequently, Mulford and his associates devised a number of instruments designed to identify "alcoholics" (141, 144, 148, 149). Although some of these have been adapted for use in field work on Indian drinking, as by Jessor et al. (87, *p. 169*) and Levy and Kunitz (113, *p. 227*), they seem less suitable for summarizing the data than Jellinek's own set of symptoms, since they are in the form of questions. In any case, the Preoccupation with Alcohol Scale, which Mulford and Miller felt identified alcoholics and heavy drinkers most accurately (148, *p. 682*), was based on Jellinek's symptoms (149, *p. 2*) and is not as detailed; it covers only 10 of the 43 symptoms included by Jellinek, plus three additional items (149, *p. 3*).

Jellinek's symptoms were derived exclusively from the behavior reported by men. Sex differences in drinking norms seem to exist in

[1]See Cooperative Commission (26, *p. 41*).

most cultures; Mandelbaum (124, *p. 282*) says perhaps in all cultures. Women almost always drink less than men. Jellinek (81,*p.676*) specifically pointed out that the behavior of women alcoholics differs from that of men. However, most of the generalizations in the literature on Indian drinking apply only to men; women's drinking usually is discussed separately, if at all. Therefore, the fact that Jellinek's symptoms are based on only male behavior does not restrict their usefulness for the present purpose. Subsequent generalizations herein, however, apply only to men unless women are specifically included.

The subcommittee of the World Health Organization which incorporated Jellinek's (81) criteria into its definition of alcoholism was presumably alert to ethnocentrism. Jellinek himself frequently demonstrated his own awareness of cultural differences in drinking behavior and definitions of alcoholism (e.g., 82, 84). Nevertheless, in the light of the Levy and Kunitz caveats (113, *pp. 220–221*), quoted earlier, it seems appropriate to examine the Jellinek symptoms for sources and signs of possible cultural bias.

Jellinek's set of symptoms of alcohol addiction grew out of his analysis of the responses of 98 men to a questionnaire devised and answered by members of Alcoholics Anonymous (78). The objective of the original A.A. questionnaire was not clear. Jellinek remarked (78, *p. 5*), "Frequently, when a questionnaire is decided upon, the only consideration underlying it is that we must have some information on this matter," and he implied that this may have been the case with the A.A. questionnaire. Jellinek had nothing to do with devising the questionnaire, but was asked to analyze the responses. He remarked (78, *p. 5*): "I have undertaken this work with great interest but also many misgivings. Statistical thinking should not begin after a survey or an experiment has been completed but should enter into the first plans for obtaining the data. In the questionnaire under consideration this requirement was neglected." Nevertheless, Jellinek eventually incorporated 30 of the 36 A.A. questions, almost verbatim, into a more detailed revision of the questionnaire (111 items) which he subsequently administered to about 2,000 alcoholics (81, *p. 673*). The responses provided the basis for his definition of alcohol addiction as a constellation of symptoms, which I use as criteria.

Thus, Jellinek's symptoms were based in part on items which had been identified by recovered alcohol addicts as useful in recognizing other addicts. Anthropologists will detect the element of ethno-science methodology in this approach.

All social scientists will surely recognize the possible bias result-ing from the use of characteristics of A.A. members as norms. Data on this group suggest that the members by no means represent a cross-section of the alcohol addicts in the general population, let alone in subgroups thereof.[2] Jellinek acknowledged this fact when he spoke of those types of alcohol addicts "who are attracted to A.A." (78, p. 6) and when he complained that American ideas about "alcoholism" and "alcoholics" have been "created by Alcoholics Anonymous in their own image" (84, p. 35).

Jellinek did not elaborate on the differences between alcoholics who join A.A. and those who do not, but subsequent studies have done so. For example, samples of A.A. members have been found to hold jobs of higher status (193, p. 320) and to exhibit a stronger "need to establish and maintain positive affective relations" (193, p. 319) than control groups of non-A.A. alcoholics. In the absence of evidence to the contrary, we must suspect that in many character-istics Jellinek's A.A. group, from which he derived an important segment of his "norms," differed significantly from non-A.A. alcohol addicts of the dominant society, and perhaps even more from can-didates for the label addict who are members of subcultures such as Indians.

In addition to the symptoms derived from his A.A. questionnaire, Jellinek included a few others, presumably abstracted from his own observations of people he considered to be alcohol addicts. We have no way of knowing how representative that sample might be of addicts in general.

Jellinek divided his list of symptoms into three developmental phases: prodromal, crucial and chronic. He (81, p. 676) explicitly warned that "Not all symptoms . . . occur necessarily in all alcohol addicts, nor do they occur in every addict in the same sequence. The 'phases' and the sequences of symptoms . . . represent what may be called the average trend." In his original detailed phaseology

---

[2]Trice (192, p. 40) provides a brief summary of literature to 1957 on the differences between alcoholics who affiliate with A.A. and those who do not. Pittman and Snyder (156, p. 549) also mention this phenomenon and provide a few references. Other pertinent works include Lofland and Lejeune (119), Maxwell (128) and Trice (193).

article he emphasized that the order of events is often reversed, for example, depending on the subjects' age, and he provided specific examples (78, *pp.* 77–78). He further pointed out that the onset and duration of at least two behaviors, solitary drinking and anti-social acts, are not restricted to a particular phase (78, *p.* 73), and said that "Certain social experiences were felt by some . . . at an early stage and by others at much later stages."

Thus, Jellinek took great pains to warn that the phases of alcohol addiction he depicted should be regarded as an average course of events for the sample from which they were derived, rather than as a universal blueprint for any and every addict's experience. Therefore, criticisms on the grounds that the phases are not strictly applicable to all addicts—recent examples quoted in Cahalan (17, *p. 4*)—seem unfair. On the other hand, efforts to refine Jellinek's "average"—e.g., Trice and Wahl's (194) analysis that more adequately reveals clustering and individual variations—are appropriate. However, neither the division of symptoms into phases nor the sequence of symptoms within each phase is crucial to the argument here.

On the other hand, in our search for signs of possible ethnocentric bias in Jellinek's symptoms, we must address a related criticism. Cahalan (17, *p.* 4) says:

"Jellinek's . . . conceptions appear to have been subtly influenced by the Protestant ethic. His phases of alcohol addiction, with its orderly—and, inferentially, irreversible—progression of malign symptoms . . . is of a piece with Hogarth's famous illustration of a drunkard's progress on the downward path to perdition. While Jellinek does not say that the phases of alcohol addiction always occur in the same order, his vivid descriptions of the progress of alcoholism are so well attuned to the values of the middle-class Western physican and welfare worker that his cautions are largely overlooked by those who apply his concepts and by the many writers who repeat his early concepts."

This criticism is not really applicable to Jellinek, but only to those who have interpreted his phases and order of symptoms as irreversible, which he specifically denied.

Nevertheless, we shall see that the charge of cultural bias in Jellinek's list of symptoms seems justified. However, this should not be interpreted as a criticism of Jellinek. He never claimed that the symptoms were applicable as criteria of alcohol addiction in other cultures. Justification for using them here for such a purpose is based solely on expediency. Jellinek's (81) list of symptoms of alcohol addiction seems to be the most appropriate instrument so far available for investigating the reverse-firewater hypothesis that alcohol addiction is rare among American Indians. It merely provides a convenient framework for a discussion which concludes that more suitable criteria are required.

I shall rate the Jellinek symptoms of alcohol addiction as PRESENT, ABSENT–RARE, CONFLICTING EVIDENCE or INSUFFICIENT EVIDENCE. These ratings represent my interpretation of the balance of evidence on the occurrence of each symptom in the Indian groups covered in the literature I have consulted.

The number of works cited in justification of the ratings varies among symptoms, as comparison of the length of the supporting notes reveals. Some symptoms are discussed in almost all the works consulted. Others are mentioned in only a few. Therefore, the strength of the evidence for a particular rating is uneven among symptoms. As each symptom is discussed, the basis for the rating is described in detail.

Estimates of rates of incidence of symptoms would be necessary to determine whether they occur more (or less) frequently among the Indian groups covered than in the general population. Unfortunately, adequate data on the incidence of most of Jellinek's symptoms of alcohol addiction are not available for either group. I have had to substitute the crude gauge of PRESENT VS ABSENT–RARE. But even the latter rating implies more information on relative incidence than the literature really affords; however, I have assigned this rating only when observers give the strong impression that they believe the incidence of a symptom among Indians is markedly less than in the general population. The rating PRESENT has been assigned when an author seems to suggest a rate of incidence at least equal to that in the general population. Nevertheless, given the nature of the data available on both groups, my ratings involve as much interpretation as reporting.

The ratings of the occurrence of symptoms of alcohol addiction are based mainly on works which focus on Indian drinking. In a few cases, I have also used statements from personal correspondence with some of the authors of these studies. Of course, many general ethnographies include material on Indian alcohol use. I have not attempted to survey this extensive literature systematically. The ethnographic works cited herein are either (a) referred to in studies of drinking, including some which have been cited from the Human

Relations Area Files data—e.g., Bacon et al. (2), Horton (71) and Washburne (208)—(b) have been particularly commended to me by scholars specializing in the subject of Indian drinking as containing data relevant to the occurrence of Jellinek's symptoms of alcohol addiction, or (c) have been included because I have noticed that the author expresses an opinion about the incidence of "alcoholism" in an Indian group.

The type and scope of the literature consulted varies widely. Books, monographs, journal articles of varying length, professional papers, speeches, newspaper accounts, popular articles, reports and proposals to funding agencies and governmental bodies, and personal correspondence all have been cited in support of various symptom ratings. I believe the nature of each work is sufficiently clear from the bibliographic entries to enable the reader to take it into account in evaluating my generalizations when this aspect of a particular symptom rating is not discussed.

The theoretical orientations of the authors cited represent a wide range of disciplines and professions, as indicated in brackets after the authors' names in the bibliography. Where reasonable effort has not enabled me to identify an author's field and level of specialization I have substituted information which seems pertinent to his qualifications, such as his position and organization, to facilitate critical evaluation of my generalizations.

The studies cited in support of the symptom ratings include some which report conditions prior to 1940, and a number which deal with early days of White contact. Such works have in no case provided the sole basis for the rating of a symptom, and are included only to document the antiquity of the drinking practice in question. In Dailey's opinion (28, p. 25), "the pattern of use remains traditional" among North American Indians, despite variation in the beverage used and in the apparent objective of drinking. However, I do not rely on his opinion as justification for including historical works in documenting the occurrence of symptoms, since no conclusions are drawn from the antiquity of the drinking practices, nor are "modern" and "historical" drinking behaviors compared.

Even among the modern studies (a term I use to describe those made since 1940, which includes the majority of 20th century studies focusing on Indian drinking), the appropriateness of comparing data gathered 20 or 30 years apart is open to challenge. However, in one of the few available comparisons of a group over time, Heath

(63) reports that Navaho drinking practices have remained remarkably stable over several decades, despite noteworthy changes in conditions, such as the repeal of federal and state prohibition of liquor sales to Indians. Nevertheless, conditions for some groups may have changed markedly since a particular study cited was made. This is a familiar problem in comparative studies of any kind. We must work with the data we have. However, it is necessary to be alert to possible bias from the variation in time among the modern studies cited. The time period covered by each of the works cited in support of symptom ratings is designated as "historical" or "modern" (or both), as defined above, in columns 3 and 4 of the Appendix.

The works on which I base symptom ratings cover only a small portion of the Indian groups in the United States and Canada. The name of the group has been added in brackets at the end of the bibliographic citation if it is not obvious from the title. For convenience in comparisons, I have also prepared a cross-reference in the Appendix. Column 1 lists the groups covered, by culture area, based on Driver and Massey (37). Column 2 indicates the works from which supporting citations for each group have been drawn. Some interpretation of the level of generalization intended by the author has sometimes been required, and appears in Column 1. For example, the title of a work may refer to "Indians of the Southwest," while the contents are restricted to one or more tribes, or portions thereof. Although for brevity's sake I occasionally will refer to "Indians," I do not mean to include all North American Indians under this term, but only those groups listed in Column 1 of the Appendix. The literature provides some precedents[3] for treating a composite of "Indian drinkers" as a unit of analysis. Nevertheless, I have stopped short of this level of generalization, and use the term "Indian" merely as shorthand for "Indian men of the groups covered in the literature cited."

Most of the works cited contain observations of drinking practices in one or, at most, a few Indian groups. They deal for the most part

---

[3]Akwesasne Notes (223); American Indian workshop (222); Boyce (13); Dailey (28); Dozier (36); Fahy and Muschenheim (40); Tax, cit. Geyer (54); von Hentig (66); MacAndrew and Edgerton (121); McKinley (123); Martinez (127); Reifel (161); Sanchez (168); Spindler and Spindler (181); and U.S.H.E.W. (198), generalize to "Indian" drinking behavior. Stewart (184) emphasizes the relationship between alcohol use and "American Indian" criminality.

with normative behavior, and do not attempt to describe the total range of behavior surrounding alcohol use. The extremes of abstinence and "excessive drinking" (however that term is defined in the group concerned) usually receive less attention than behavior between these extremes. Few of the studies attempt systematic cross-cultural comparisons of alcohol use. The difficulties involved in generalizing from studies of individual groups are well known to anthropologists and will not be elaborated here. Such generalizations usually serve at least one useful purpose—they quickly elicit evidence to the contrary.

Based on pertinent literature, it is my opinion that the degree of homogeneity in the drinking practices of North American Indians remains a question to be investigated, although the drinking patterns as described in the literature so far present a remarkably consistent picture, with important exceptions which will be noted.

When I state that "Indians do thus and so" or "behave in X fashion" I do not pretend to be describing what they actually do, or what I believe they do, only what observers have reported they do.

The persons designated "Indian" in the literature consulted are in general self-defined as such, mainly by affiliation with a particular tribal group. Even on reservations, the blood quantum may vary from full to a small fraction. Stewart says (184, *p. 61*), "The practical advantages of being listed officially on tribal rolls are such that nearly all who can qualify are anxious to maintain their legal status as Indians." Dozier (36, *p. 74*) agrees. Therefore, it seems that a person rarely would be legally defined as "Indian" and deny it. In any case, such persons presumably would not be covered in the literature cited. On the other hand, some people who do not enjoy legal status as Indians may nevertheless claim Indian descent, and might be included in the literature on "Indian" drinking. As already discussed in the context of challenges to the firewater myth, "Indians" represent a social rather than a biological category.

The literature cited covers *(1)* Indian reservations and other nonurban Indian communities of varying degrees of isolation; (2) mixed nonurban communities in which Indians represent varying proportions of the total population; and (3) groups of urban Indians of one or more tribal origins. The type of community emphasized by individual studies is indicated in columns 5–8 of the Appendix.

Theoretically, we would expect behavior, drinking or otherwise, to vary greatly among such diverse communities. On many points, however, the literature depicts drinking patterns of urban and non-urban Indians as more similar than different. This is my justification for lumping them in this study, except where specific differences have been noted. However, I suspect that a great deal more data would be required to establish the degree of similarity in the drinking behavior of Indian communities of varying size and urbanization.

The literature cited in support of symptom ratings varies greatly along all the dimensions just discussed. Such variation is in turn a factor in judging the relative "quality" of a work for the purpose at hand. The heterogeneity already described seems to preclude any formal ranking for use in assigning relative weight to the evidence provided in particular studies. The explanation and justification for such a ranking system would require more space than seems appropriate here. In my opinion, however, the data on Indian drinking in the literature on which this study is based vary greatly in quality, both among works and within a particular work. This judgment has undoubtedly entered, however informally or unconsciously, into my ratings of the occurrence of symptoms.

The "evidence" used consists largely of inferences made by the observers. The data from which these inferences are drawn are seldom presented in great detail. Many of the statements relied upon are rather cursory generalizations which are seldom adequate for a refined approach to an investigation of the reverse-firewater hypothesis.

In short, the generalizations in this study represent my interpretation of the balance of evidence of varying quality from an extremely heterogeneous body of works on drinking in a number of North American Indian groups.

The approach used in evaluating the reverse-firewater hypothesis is briefly outlined below:

1. The scattered "evidence" on topics pertinent to an evaluation of the reverse-firewater hypothesis will be compiled and analyzed as the basis for *rating the occurrence of symptoms of alcohol addiction* in the Indian groups covered. The four rating categories are PRESENT, AB:ENT-RARE, CONFLICTING EVIDENCE, and INSUFFICIENT EVIDENCE (Chapter 4). The ratings of all the symptoms are summarized in Table 1 at the beginning of Chapter 4.

2. The symptom ratings will be summarized in a *tally of symptom*

ratings; in the process, problems of weighting and interpretation will be discussed (Chapter 5).

3. Since the results of the foregoing tally are indecisive, a weaker alternative test of the reverse-firewater hypothesis is attempted—a *tally of opinion* on the occurrence among Indians of "alcohol addiction," regardless of the criteria on which the opinions are based. The results of this second tally are also indecisive (Chapter 6).

4. The *reverse-firewater hypothesis is labeled "myth,"* at least in the sense of "undocumented," and, until data are available for an adequate test, it is concluded that the hypothesis may merit another connotation of the term "myth," i.e., false. Some possible explanations for the lack of consensus in the literature are briefly discussed and suggestions for future work are offered (Chapter 7).

4

Symptoms of Alcohol Addiction

EVIDENCE from the literature on Indian drinking concerning the occurrence among Indians of a set of symptoms of alcohol addiction, based on Jellinek (81), is summarized in this chapter. On the basis of this evidence, each of these symptoms is assigned a rating in one of the following categories: PRESENT, ABSENT-RARE, CONFLICTING EVIDENCE, or INSUFFICIENT EVIDENCE. These ratings are summarized in Table 1. It should be emphasized that the ratings of occurrence of these symptoms apply only to the Indian groups covered in the literature cited.

1. Alcoholic Palimpsests: INSUFFICIENT EVIDENCE

The term palimpsest is derived from the Greek for "scraped again" and refers to materials such as slate which can be used, erased, and used again, or to manuscripts which have been written on such material. The word is used in alcohol studies to refer to "blackouts," which Jellinek (81, *p. 678*) describes as follows:

"The drinker who may have had not more than 50 to 60 g. of absolute alcohol and who is not showing any signs of intoxication may carry on a reasonable conversation or may go through quite elaborate activities without a trace of memory the next day, although sometimes one or two minor details may be hazily remembered."

The process leading to this amnesia is little understood. Jellinek (81, *p. 678*) hypothesized that a malutilization of oxygen may be involved, but he acknowledged that palimpsests could have a psychological rather than a physiological basis.

To qualify as indicators of alcohol addiction, Jellinek (81, *p. 678*) says palimpsests must occur "frequently" and after "medium alcohol intake." Jellinek provides no standard for "frequent." From his statement quoted above, I suppose we can assume that "medium" intake is in the range of 50 or 60 grams of alcohol, equal to about 4 oz of distilled spirits at average strength.

Few observers of Indian drinking explicitly mention blackouts.

In isolated cases (e.g., 58, *p. 293;* 165, *p. 51*) the occurrence of black-outs might be inferred from the behavior reported. Three observers report that blackouts while drinking occur in the groups on which they report. In populations of Indians jailed for drunkenness, black-outs have been reported by 77% of the Navaho (48, *p. 907*) and 71% of the Uintah-Ouray (239, *p. 20*). In a random sample of the Stand-ing Rock Sioux Tribe, 42% reported having experienced blackouts (212, *p. 475*).

However, as Keller points out,[1] survey questions intended to elicit information about alcoholic palimpsests are often imprecisely word-ed in terms of "forgetting," and control groups are not asked whether they forget what happened the night before—without drinking.

Nevertheless, even if we assume that the manifestations cited above really are blackouts, mere occurrence does not enable us to know whether they occur in a manner which would qualify as symp-tomatic of alcohol addiction in Jellinek's terms. Only two of the observers who report the occurrence of blackouts provide some in-dication of frequency. Of Slater's Uintah-Ouray arrested popula-tion (239, *p. 20*), 12% reported having experienced blackouts "often," and 25% of those who reported blackouts in Whittaker's Standing Rock Sioux general population sample (212, *p. 475*) admitted "fre-quent" occurrence. However, we do not have a standard of "fre-quent" or "often," either from Jellinek or from these Indian informants.

Berreman (10, *p. 511*) indicated that, although blackouts do oc-cur among members of an Aleut group, "no individual repeatedly and continually displayed" this symptom. Jellinek does not require that blackouts be "continual" to qualify as symptoms of alcohol ad-diction, but his description clearly implies that they must occur "repeatedly" in one individual. Assuming that Jellinek and Berre-man share a common standard for "repeatedly," the blackouts re-ported in the Aleuts would not seem to qualify as symptoms of alco-hol addiction.

None of the observers who report the occurrence of blackouts in an Indian group estimate the quantity of intake which precedes manifestation of the symptom, to enable comparison with Jellinek's standard of not more than 50 to 60 grams of absolute alcohol.

Several authors say they have noticed a discrepancy between the amount drunk and the degree of intoxication exhibited by Indians

[1]Keller, M. Personal communication, 15 March 1972.

TABLE 1

TABLE 1.—*Summary of Ratings of Occurrence of Jellinek Symptoms of Alcohol Addiction among North American Indian Groups*

SYMPTOMS	Present	Absent or Rare	Conflicting Evidence	Insufficient Evidence
Prodromal Phase				
1. Alcoholic palimpsests (blackouts)				x
2. Surreptitious drinking				x
3. Preoccupation with alcohol				x
4. Avid drinking	x			
5. Guilt feelings about drinking behavior		x		
6. Avoid reference to alcohol				x
7. Increasing frequency of blackouts				x
Crucial Phase				
8. Loss of control				x
9. Rationalize drinking behavior				x
10. Social pressures (countered)		x		
11. Grandiose behavior				x
12. Marked aggressive behavior			x	
13. Persistent remorse				x
14. Periods of total abstinence				x
15. Changing pattern of drinking				x
16. Drop friends				x
16A. Solitary drinking			x	
17. Quit jobs				x
18. Behavior becomes alcohol-centered				x
19. Loss of outside interests				x
20. Reinterpret interpersonal relationships			x	
21. Marked self-pity				x
22. Geographic escape				x
23. Change in habits (of family)				x
24. Unreasonable resentments				x
25. Protect liquor supply				x

[cont.]

TABLE 1—*cont.*

	Pres-ent	Absent or Rare	Conflict-ing Evi-dence	Insuffi-cient Evidence
26. Neglect of proper nutrition				x
27. Hospitalization: alcoholic cirrhosis	x			
28. Decrease in sexual drive				x
29. Alcoholic jealousy				x
30. Regular matutinal drinking				x
Chronic Phase				
31. Prolonged intoxications	x			
32. Marked ethical deterioration				x
33. Impairment of thinking				x
34. Alcoholic psychoses				x
35. Drinks with persons below social level				x
36. Recourse to "technical products"				x
37. Loss of alcohol tolerance				x
38. Indefinable fears				x
39. Tremors				x
40. Psychomotor inhibition				x
41. Drinking takes on obsessive character				x
42. Vague religious desires develop				x
43. Rationalization system fails				x
Totals	3	2	3	36

they have observed, or imply as much by suggesting that the subjects may feign drunkenness.[2] Lemert (108, *p. 98*) postulates that Indians may deliberately pretend intoxication to act out the White stereotype of the drunken Indian. Hurt and Brown (74, *p. 229*) report feigned drunkenness which they attribute to the tabu against arriving at a party sober. Some Indians may act more intoxicated than they really are in anticipation of becoming drunk, which is often said to be the

[2]Berreman (10, *pp. 507, 508*); Dailey (28, *p. 26*); Devereux (33, *p. 227*); Heath (62, *p. 68*); Hurt and Brown (74, *p. 228*); Koolage (99, *p. 112*); Lemert (108, *pp. 97–98*); Robbins (162, *p. 163*); Slotkin (175, *p. 12*).

explicit objective of drinking by many Indians.[3] Or, intoxication on small amounts of alcohol actually could occur, for example, as a consequence of certain aspects of the predominant style of drinking among Indians, such as rapid intake (see Symptom 4).

Even if it were established that Indians do become intoxicated on relatively small amounts of alcohol, this would tell us nothing about the quantity required to bring on blackouts. I interject this subject here only to suggest that Jellinek's standard of quantity might be difficult to apply among Indians even if data on amounts they consume were available.

This discussion of alcoholic palimpsests illustrates several problems encountered in investigating the incidence of alcohol addiction among Indians. First, mere evidence of "occurrence" is inadequate; data on individual and group rates, and sometimes other details such as the quantity of intake preceding the symptom, would be required before we could judge whether a symptom occurs among Indians in a way that really meets Jellinek's criteria of alcohol addiction. Second, the data on dominant-society drinkers are often inadequate to provide a standard for comparison. Third, even when we are provided with absolute standards for comparison, special circumstances among Indians may make them difficult to use for the purpose at hand.

Kunitz[4] has pointed out that blackouts are to be expected, given the binge style of drinking most often documented among Indian groups (see Symptom 8). However, blackouts are mentioned in only a small portion of the groups in the literature cited. Of course, lack of evidence cannot be interpreted as negative evidence. It may simply reflect the difficulty of observing a phenomenon such as blackouts. Even in the groups in which blackouts reportedly do occur, the evidence so far is insufficient to enable determination whether they occur in a manner which would qualify as symptomatic of addiction.

[3]Balikci (7, p. 197); Berreman (10, p. 507); Brody (16, pp. 35-36); Carpenter (19, p. 151); Curley (27, p. 121); Dailey (28, pp. 23, 25); Ferguson (47, p. 162; 48, p. 901); Hamer (59, p. 233); Hawthorn et al. (61, p. 11); Heath (62, pp. 33, 37; 63, pp. 127, 131); Honigmann and Honigmann (68, p. 590); Horton (71, p. 260) [Naskapi and Papago]; Howay (72, p. 166); Lemert (107, pp. 310, 317; 108, pp. 91, 93, 99); Martinez (127, p. 2); Maynard (129, p. 38); Rohner and Rohner (165, p. 47); Vachon (203, p. 22); Whittaker (212, p. 478).

[4]Kunitz, S. J. Personal communication, 25 May 1971.

2. Surreptitious Drinking: INSUFFICIENT EVIDENCE

Jellinek (81, *pp. 678–679*) described surreptitious drinking as follows:

"At social gatherings the drinker seeks occasions for having a few drinks unknown to others, as he fears that if it were known that he drinks more than the others he would be misjudged: those to whom drinking is only a custom or a small pleasure would not understand that because he is different from them alcohol is for him a necessity, although he is not a drunkard."

Drinking in a number of Indian groups has been described as "surreptitious." The concealment, however, is usually from police,[5] priests (107, *p. 373;* 108, *p. 92*), or uninvited guests,[6] rather than from companions, family or community, which Jellinek seems to have had in mind. On the contrary, several authors report that drinking in a number of Indian groups is notably public.[7] However, Levy and Kunitz (113, *p. 232*), on the basis of Hopi evidence, suspect that covert drinking may be more widespread than the literature has indicated, at least in that group, and may have been overlooked simply because it is less visible than public drinking. Earlier, Horton (71, *p. 266*) noted evidence of surreptitious drinking, apparently in Jellinek's sense, among the H.R.A.F. accounts of Hopi and Zuni alcohol use. Indeed certain Hopi characteristics, to be discussed later, suggest that such behavior might more likely occur among them than among other groups.

Concerning the majority of groups covered in the literature cited, surreptitious drinking as defined by Jellinek is not reported. On the other hand, its occurrence is not explicitly denied.

3. Preoccupation with Alcohol: INSUFFICIENT EVIDENCE

Jellinek (81, *p. 679*) included this symptom among several drinking behaviors (Symptoms 2, 5 and 6) which indicate that for the person

[5]Boyer (14, *p. 217*); Curley (27, *p. 119*); Ferguson (47, *pp. 160, 162*); Geertz (230, *p. 102*); Hawthorn et al. (61, *p. 10*); Heath (62, *pp. 16, 33, 37, 72;* 63, *pp. 125, 131*); Honigmann and Honigmann (68, *pp. 590, 615*); Horton (71, *p. 266*); Indian Affairs (225, *p. 3*); Lemert (107, *p. 373;* 108, *p. 93*); Martinez (127, *p. 3*); Robbins (162, *p. 151*).

[6]Balikci (7, *p. 196*); Hawthorn et al. (61, *p. 10*); Mindell (237, *p. 4*); Robbins (162, *p. 151*).

[7]Collins (25, *p. 126*), "poor" households; Ferguson (46, *p. 2;* 47, *p. 161*); Hawthorn et al. (61, *p. 11*); Jessor (86, *p. 69*); Lemert (107, *p. 316*); Littman (117, *p. 1770*); Martinez (127, *p. 2*); Meier (131, *p. 119*).

who exhibits them alcohol has ceased to be a beverage and has
become a drug which he "needs." Jellinek (81, *p. 679*) describes
preoccupation with alcohol as follows:

"When he first prepares to go to a social gathering his first thought is
whether there will be sufficient alcohol for his requirements, and he has
several drinks in anticipation of a possible shortage."

When Indians cannot easily obtain liquor, either because of local
prohibition, remoteness from outlets, or lack of funds, there appears
to be a good deal of maneuvering to secure or brew a supply; and,
once a binge has begun, rather elaborate measures are taken to
obtain more drink to continue the party.[8] Whatever preoccupation
with alcohol such behavior might suggest would appear to be ex-
plainable by circumstances. The preparty fortification and implied
individual dependence on alcohol which Jellinek uses as criteria are
not necessarily motivating factors. On the contrary, some accounts
of Indian alcohol use, as by Berreman (10, *p. 512*) and Lemert (107,
p. 362), give the impression that the groups described may be notably unpreoccupied with liquor; when alcohol is available, there is
a party; when it is not, no one becomes upset by the lack.

More systematic attempts to measure preoccupation with alcohol,
however, as by Levy and Kunitz (114, *pp. 146-151*) in samples of
Navaho Indians, suggest that this symptom might well occur in
this group. These observers used a Preoccupation with Alcohol
Scale adapted from one used by Jessor et al. (87), which was based
on Mulford and Wilson (149). As already mentioned, the latter
scale consists of several items treated as separate symptoms by Jellinek. In addition to these, the scale includes intoxication on work
days, drinking for effect with little regard for the type or quality
of beverage consumed, and increased alcohol tolerance (149, *p. 3*).
Thus the Mulford and Wilson Preoccupation with Alcohol Scale
measures the incidence of far more symptoms than Jellinek's preparty fortification. Levy and Kunitz (114, *p. 150*) report that most
of the Navaho drinkers scored in the so-called alcoholic range on the
preoccupation scale. A similar pattern had been reported earlier
from two smaller samples of Hopis (113, *p. 233*). Among the
Navaho, they found that high preoccupation with alcohol was correlated negatively with degree of acculturation, in agreement with
the findings of Jessor et al. (87) in the Southern Ute in a southwest-

[8]E.g., Clairmont (22, *p. 2*); Curley (27, *p. 121*); Lemert (108, *p. 96*).

ern triethnic community. The proportion of male drinkers who reported behavior yielding scores identified by Mulford and his associates as indicating "alcoholism" ranged from 25% of the most acculturated group to 70% of the least acculturated. Thus, in the group as a whole, a minimum of 25% exhibited preoccupation with alcohol to a degree that Mulford interpreted as indicating the presence of alcoholism. In Mulford and Wilson's sample in Cedar Rapids, Iowa (149, *p. 9*), only 5% of the general population scored in this range. This would seem to indicate that among the Navaho, the incidence of whatever is measured by the Preoccupation with Alcohol Scale is high compared to a limited sample from the general population. However, Levy and Kunitz (114, *p. 148*) point out that although items in the scale which best identified White alcoholics also pick out a group of Navaho self-referred alcoholics, they do not distinguish between them and a group of Navahos not regarded as alcoholics.[9]

Strictly speaking, only the responses to the equivalent of Mulford's item "I worry about not being able to get a drink when I need one" would seem to correspond to Jellinek's description of the symptom "preoccupation with alcohol." The analyses of the responses so far published by Levy and Kunitz do not include separate scores for the individual test questions, but provide total test scores only (114, *pp. 146–151* and Appendix IV). In any case, on the remaining groups covered in the literature, we have inadequate data for rating the occurrence of the symptom as defined by Jellinek.

Even if we adopt the broader definition suggested by Mulford the results remain ambiguous, except perhaps for the Navaho. If we break down that scale into the items treated as separate symptoms by Jellinek, we find that 5 (Symptoms 1, 2, 3, 8, 26) have been rated herein as INSUFFICIENT EVIDENCE and only 3 (Symptoms 4, 27, 31) have been rated PRESENT (Table 1). Thus, the available evidence is insufficient to rate the occurrence of this symptom among Indians with either Jellinek's or Mulford's definition.

4. Avid Drinking: PRESENT

Jellinek (81, *p. 679*) described avid drinking as "gulping the first or the first two drinks."

The literature suggests that rapid drinking is standard drinking

---

[9]This intriguing complication has been discussed by Levy and Kunitz (114, *p. 148*).

style in many Indian groups.[10] Maynard (129, *p. 38*) notes that among the Oglala Sioux avid drinking is not even restricted to problem drinkers. Furthermore, gulping does not seem to be confined to the first drinks, but continues until the party ends.

Avid drinking is probably a natural accompaniment of drinking to get drunk, documented under Symptom 1 as characteristic of many Indians. After all, drinking fast is the most efficient way to achieve this objective, provided the drinker does not become sick or unconscious in the meantime.

If rapid drinking is the normal style in a particular Indian group, can it be considered a symptom of addiction, which is by definition deviant? The apparent paradox is resolved if we define the relativistic framework, i.e., the WHO's "whole community concerned," to include the dominant society, in which avid drinking is regarded as deviant. But this underscores the difficulty of using a relativistic definition of alcohol addiction. If alcohol addiction is to be wholly culturally defined, the appropriate frame of reference would seem to be the individual Indian group, not the general population. If the "community concerned" were defined as Indians of the Western Hemisphere,[11] then we might be tempted to conclude that avid drinking is modal for the group, and thus could not be considered a sign of deviant drinking in that frame of reference.

There is a further difficulty in considering avid drinking as a symptom of alcohol addiction in North American Indian groups. A number of authors[12] have pointed out that prohibition (which continues today on many reservations, tribally imposed) encourages avid drinking, since it influences the drinker to finish his bottle before he is caught with the incriminating evidence. Furthermore, the charge of possession usually results in a harsher sentence than mere

[10]Balikci (*7, p. 196*); Clairmont (*22, p. 2*); Curley (*27, pp. 121, 126*); Dailey (*28, p. 23; 29, p. 48*); Devereux (*33, p. 209*); Ferguson (*46, p. 2; 47, p. 163, 48, pp. 900, 907*); Geertz (*230, p. 102*); Hamer (*58, p. 290*); Hawthorn et al. (*61, p. 11*); Heath (*63, pp. 125, 131*); Honigmann and Honigmann, (*70, p. 75*); Hurt and Brown (*74, p. 223*); IHS Task Force (*75, p. 4*); Jessor (*86, p. 69*); Lemert (*107, pp. 307, 310, 317; 108, pp. 91, 93, 99*); Martinez (*127, p. 2*); Rohner and Rohner (*165, p. 46*); Sanchez (*168, p. 1*); Toler (*191, p. 2*).

[11]See Mandelbaum (*124, p. 285*) for a description of Central and South American drinking patterns which seem to be characteristic of broad areas.

[12]E. g., Curley (*27, p. 118*); Devereux (*33, p. 209*); Ferguson (*47, p. 163*); Geertz (*230, p. 102*); Heath (*62, p. 75*); Hawthorn et al. (*61, p. 11*); Lemert (*107, p. 357*); Martinez (*127, p. 2*).

drunkenness,[13] and this encourages fast drinking.[14] In such cases, circumstances may account for the avid drinking; individual dependence on alcohol, which underlies Jellinek's interpretation of rapid drinking as a symptom of alcohol addiction, is not necessarily involved. On the other hand, even in border towns and urban centers where there is no prohibition, authors who document speed of intake report that avid drinking is the modal style (e.g., 63, *pp. 125, 131; 86, p. 69*).

The primary task here is to rate the occurrence of the behaviors Jellinek described. The problems involved in interpreting the occurrence of such behaviors among Indians as symptomatic of alcohol addiction are further discussed in Chapter 5. Of the studies which report that avid drinking (Symptom 4) is PRESENT in the groups covered, 16 qualify as "accounts" [15] in support of the symptom rating (Table 2). The "accounts" include at least 1 group in 6 of the 9 culture areas represented in the literature on Indian alcohol use, as shown in Table 2. A majority of these "accounts" refer to all-Indian settlements, but Indians who live in racially mixed communities, both nonurban and urban, are also represented (cf. Appendix).

[13]Curley (27, *p. 118*); Dailey (28, *p. 23*); Szuter et al. (187, *p. 1*).

[14]Curley (27, *p. 126*); Dailey (28, *p. 23*); Devereux (33, *p. 209*); Dozier (36, *p. 84*); Ferguson (46, *p. 2; 47, p. 163*); Geertz (230, *p. 102*); Graves (57, *p. 38*); Hawthorn et al. (61, *p. 11*); Heath (62, *pp. 33, 37, 72; 63, p. 125*); Kilen (236, *p. 2*); Lemert (107, *pp. 357, 373*); Rohner and Rohner (165, *p. 47*); Sanchez (168, *p. 2*); Toler (191, *p. 2*).

[15]The following procedure has been followed in calculating the number of supporting "accounts" of each of the 5 symptoms which have received a definite rating of PRESENT or ABSENT-RARE shown in Table 2. The number of "accounts" is derived from pertinent citations in footnotes and the text. Some of these are excluded, however, on the following grounds. Reports by one author (or a set of joint authors) constitute a single "account" even though a symptom is rated thereby in more than one group or in more than one study. The purpose of this rule is to avoid giving undue weight to a few authors. Supporting "accounts" which refer only to the "historical" period as defined herein (i.e., pre-1940) are not included in the calculations or, hence, in Table 2, because our main interest is in the modern period. The Appendix indicates the era covered by each of the groups cited in supporting citations. However, some of those which qualify as "accounts" refer to both the historical and the modern era; in these cases I have judged from context which era the statement cited in support of the rating actually refers to. The calculation of the number of "accounts" which qualify as supporting symptom ratings can in each case be verified in Table 2, which also shows the distribution across culture areas—as defined by Driver and Massey (37)—of the groups covered in the qualifying

TABLE 2.—*Summary of Culture Area Distribution of Symptoms of Alcohol Addiction Rated* PRESENT *or* ABSENT–RARE[a]

CULTURE AREA[b]	4	5	10	27	31
Arctic Coast					
Aleut of Nikolski		A	A		P
Eskimo of Kaktovik			A		
Eskimo of Aklavik	P		A		P
Eskimo of Frobisher Bay	P				
Eskimo, etc., of Mackenzie Delta			A	(1)[d]	P
Subarctic					
Vunta Kutchin	P			(1)[d]	
Kaska of "Delio"		A	A	(1)[d]	
Chipewyan, etc. of Churchill, Manitoba			A		P
Naskapi			A		P
Northwest Coast					
3 Salish tribes	P}(1)	A}(1)	A}(1)		P}
Kwakiutl	P		A		
Bella Coola		A			
Plateau					
Klamath			A		P
Plains					
Kiowa Apache					P
Oglala Sioux				A	[cont.]

"accounts." The information on culture area can be cross-checked by comparing the assignment of the pertinent groups in the Appendix. In addition to the culture areas, both Table 2 and the Appendix include two other categories: *(1)* "Indians of North America," in which are classified the "accounts" which I have interpreted as intending a generalization at this level; and *(2)* "Miscellaneous," in which I have classified the "accounts" which refer to groups in more than one culture area. Generalizations in the text about community type can be verified by cross-checking in the Appendix the name of the pertinent groups in Table 2.

I will illustrate this procedure, using Avid drinking (Symptom 4) as an example. Footnote 10 cites 23 reports indicating that Avid drinking is PRESENT in the groups to which they refer. Citations (107) and (108) constitute a single "account," because they are by the same author, as indicated by the braces enclosing the symbol "P" (for PRESENT) after 'Northwest Coast" and its subgroup "3 Salish tribes" in Table 2. This reduces the number of "accounts"

TABLE 2.—*cont.*

	Symptom Number[c]				
	4	5	10	27	31
Prairies					
Sioux					
miscellaneous			A		
Standing Rock		A	A		P
Yankton of Yankton, S.D.	P	A	A		P
Menomini of Zoar		A	A		P
Potawatomi of "Whitehorse"	P	A	A		P
Indians in Omaha		A	A		
Desert					
Southern Ute	P		A (2)		
Uintah-Ouray Northern Ute		A	A (3)	P	P
Indians of Nevada		A			
Oasis					
Apache					
Mescalero	P	A	A (2)		P
White Mountain				P⎫(1)	
Hopi				P⎭	P
Navaho	P (3)	A	A (5)	P (3)	P (4)
"New Mexico Tribes"	P (2)				
Mohave	P		A		
"Indians," probably Oasis only			A		
Indians of North America		A (2)	A (3)	P (3)	P (2)
Miscellaneous					
(several culture areas represented)	P	A (2)	A		P
Unknown					P
Total number of accounts	16	17	34	8	23

ᵃ P = present; A = absent-rare. See footnote 15, Chapter 4.

ᵇ The nine culture areas of Driver and Massey (37) are Arctic Coast, Subarctic, Northwest Coast, Plateau, Plains, Prairies, East, Desert, and Oasis. East is omitted from this Table.

ᶜ 4 = avid drinking, footnote 15; 5 = guilt feelings about drinking behavior, footnote 18; 10 = social pressures (countered), footnote 55; 27 = hospitalization (alcoholic cirrhosis), footnote 91; 31 = prolonged intoxications, footnote 99.

ᵈ Numbers in parentheses indicate total number of accounts for indicated group. Citations joined by braces constitute single accounts.

to 22. On the same grounds, citations (46), (47) and (48) constitute a single "account" (reducing the number to 20), which is combined with two others concerning the Navaho, to arrive at the total of 3 qualifying "accounts" shown

5. Guilt Feelings about Drinking Behavior: ABSENT–RARE

Jellinek (81, p. 679) says, "As the drinker realizes, at least vaguely, that his drinking is outside the ordinary, he develops guilt feelings about his drinking behavior." Jellinek did not describe behavior which he would interpret as a manifestation of such guilt feelings.

Most observers report that the Indians they have studied do not feel guilty about drinking or getting drunk, or about the consequences of either.[16] For example, several authors have noted that arrests and jail sentences for drinking seem to cause less guilt and stigma among the Indians they have observed than among Whites. Thus Lemert (107, p. 356) says:

> "In none of the interviews I conducted with [Northwest Coast] Indians in prison for liquor offenses did I discover any sign of guilt or remorse on their part; the most common attitude was one of pained puzzlement over why these things are done by White men . . . some Indians released from prison have been forthwith entertained at feasts by their bands."

Littman (116, p. 69) reports, concerning Indians of varied tribal origins in Chicago, that "Most of the arrested Indians whom I interviewed admitted freely that they had been in jail for drunkenness several times in the past. Like Lemert (107, p. 356), I was not aware of any guilt or remorse on their part."

for the Navaho indicated in parentheses after the symbol "P" (PRESENT). Citations (28) and (29), which are by one author, as well as citations (75) and (168), are excluded because they report the symptom only during the "historic" period, and hence do not even appear in Table 2. This reduces the number of qualifying "accounts" to 16, as shown in the bottom line of Table 2. These are: (7), (22), (27), (33), (46, 47, & 48), (58), (61), (63), (70), (74), (86), (107 & 108), (127), (165), (191), (230).

Instead of describing this procedure in such detail for each of the 5 symptoms, I simply will indicate in a footnote the total number of citations supporting the rating, where the citations appear (i.e., footnote number or in the text), and the bibliographic entry numbers of the qualifying "accounts." Sets of numbers in parentheses qualify as single "accounts."

[16]Berreman (10, p. 512); Boyer (14, p. 234); Brody (16, pp. 33, 34); Carpenter (19, p. 149); Dailey (28, pp. 23, 25); Dozier (36, p. 83); Hamer (58, p. 291; 59, p. 238); Honigmann and Honigmann (68, pp. 591, 615); Hurt and Brown (74, pp. 223, 229); Kilen (236, p. 3); Kuttner and Lorincz (103, p. 535); Lemert (107, pp. 356–357 et seq.; 108, p. 103); Littman (116, pp. 67, 73) citing Bollinger and Starkey (227); McIlwraith (122, p. 258); Savard (169, p. 913); Slater (239, p. 7); Slotkin (175, p. 12); Thwaites (190, p. 159); Whittaker (213, p. 86).

Hawthorn et al. (61, *p. 11*) state that many Indians of British Columbia "do not seem to be unduly worried about the possibility of conviction for intoxication and this possibility does not restrain them." And Slater says (238, *p. 6*), "There doesn't seem to be the same social stigma against arrest among the [Uintah-Ouray] Indians" as in the White population.

A summary of the American Indian Workshop Session of the Utah School of Alcohol Studies reports, "There is no stigma attached to jail sentences" resulting from drinking (222, *p. 3*). So, also, von Hentig (66, *p. 83*): "No particular disgrace is attached to an arrest or a conviction" among Indians.

Even when imprisonment is not involved, there appears to be a striking absence of guilt about drinking or drunkenness among many of the Indian groups covered herein. Dailey (28, *p. 26*) comments:

"From the very beginning, reserve Indians have not associated shame and guilt with intoxication. The absence of these feelings in their personality structure has important consequences. For one thing, it accounts for why even today, the antisocial acts of drunken Indians are excused. . . . The fact that the Indian has not incorporated feelings of shame and guilt toward insobriety is one of the crucial differences between White and Indian 'alcoholics.'"

When guilt about drinking is reported to be present, it is usually specifically associated with influence from outsiders, such as missionaries or teachers,[17] or explicitly restricted to relatively acculturated individuals (e.g., 36, *p. 83*).

The Peyote cult, whose religious beliefs are in part borrowed from Christianity, apparently does attempt to instill guilt about drinking in its members (1, *p. 188*). In addition, as Dozier, for example, notes (36, *p. 85*), Indians who have been converted to Christian sects which stress the immorality of drinking are reported to have associated guilt with alcohol use, but, Dozier adds "Converts initially reject alcohol completely but adherence to the religion is typically brief."

These exceptions underscore the hazards of generalizing about

[17]American Indian Workshop (222, *p. 1*); Berreman (10, *p. 510*); Brody (16, *p. 33*); Clairmont (22, *p. 8*); Henderson (65, *pp. 64, 65*); Honigmann and Honigmann (70, *p. 78*); LaBarre (104, *p. 43*); Lemert (107, *pp. 367, 378*); Manning (125, *p. 3*); Robbins (162, *p. 157*); Szuter et al. (187, *p. 4*).

"Indians" even of a single small community, since drinking attitudes and behavior may vary within such groups.

Level of acculturation seems to bear a particularly close relationship to the incidence of the symptom "guilt about drinking behavior," although, as Lemert (107, *p. 366*) points out concerning the Northwest Coast Indians, guilt feelings about other behavior may indeed occur. He also says (107, *p. 367*):

> "My hypothesis about the form and dynamics of pathological drinking among the coastal Indians pertains to those in whom contact and interaction with White society has not brought about changes at the level of basic personality structure. Changes of this kind seem to be imminent. . . . In some of the stories I had residential school children write on the subject of 'A Person Who Got Drunk' it was possible to see the beginnings of a different attitude toward drinking which much more nearly resembled that of the surrounding White society. When and where such changes do take place, it can be judged that the forms of pathological drinking will more closely approach those found in the White Canadian and American community."

If so, we might expect an increase in the incidence of guilt about drinking behavior following a rise in level of acculturation. This hypothesis has not been systematically investigated in the literature on Indian alcohol use. A majority of the 17 "accounts" mentioning the symptom "guilt about drinking" in the literature cited herein[18] say it is ABSENT OR RARE in the modern groups they cover. As shown in Table 2, these groups represent 6 of the 9 culture areas covered in the literature on Indian drinking, plus groups consisting of Indians from several culture areas. Two of these accounts generalize about "Indians" as a whole. Indian, mixed nonurban and urban communities are all represented.

6. *Avoid Reference to Alcohol:* INSUFFICIENT EVIDENCE

Jellinek (81, *p. 679*) linked this behavior with Symptom 5, commenting that reference to alcohol is avoided "because of" guilt feelings.

Since the literature indicates that guilt about drinking seems to be absent in many of the groups reported upon, I have been tempted to

[18]Footnote 16 contains 21 citations documenting that Symptom 5 (Guilt feelings about drinking behavior) is ABSENT–RARE in the groups covered. Of these, 17 qualify as "accounts": (10), (14), (16), (28), (36), (58 and 59), (68), (74), (103), (107 and 108), (116), (122), (169), (175), (213), (236), (239).

infer that the absence of the symptom "avoid reference to alcohol" would follow. However, "guilt" is not the only possible motive for such behavior. A person might avoid the subject of alcohol because it would remind him that he has behaved inappropriately when drinking (i.e., shame), or that he has been unable to fulfill role expectations as a result of drinking (e.g., frustration, anger), even though he has no internalized conviction that such behavior is immoral (guilt). In addition, he might tabu alcohol in his conversation for strategic reasons—for example, arising from special prohibition laws (i.e., self-protection), or simply to avoid losing something he wants. Other motives might be to avoid reinforcing the drunken Indian stereotype—i.e., group pride, as suggested, for example, by Collins (25, *p. 111*), or to keep from offending an investigator who, he anticipates, may disapprove of drinking (e.g., simple courtesy). Furthermore, such behavior might simply indicate a lack of interest in alcohol, which could reflect the absence of preoccupation (Symptom 3). Data on the absence of this behavior are difficult to collect and to assess.

Even positive manifestations, i.e., data on the absence of avoiding reference to alcohol, create problems of interpretation. If an informant discusses alcohol freely, we might assume he does not suffer from this symptom of alcohol addiction as defined by Jellinek. But this behavior might also indicate the presence of preoccupation with alcohol (Symptom 3).

We might think we were getting somewhere in assessing the occurrence of this symptom in an Indian group if, for example, an observer reported a low frequency of references to alcohol in conversation and a negative correlation between the number of references to alcohol and other manifestations of problem drinking. The literature so far does not provide evidence of this kind. Even if it did, the other manifestations alone might identify the individual as a candidate for the category "alcohol addict." On the other hand, these other manifestations, or symptoms, might present the same problems of data collection as "avoid reference to alcohol."

7. *Increasing Frequency of Alcoholic Palimpsests:* INSUFFICIENT EVIDENCE

Jellinek (81, *p. 679*) provides no standard for "increasing" frequency. The evidence indicating mere presence or absence of blackouts is decidedly sparse. The literature provides even less information on the frequency of occurrence among individuals, as I pointed out in the previous discussion of this subject (Symptom 1). I have encountered only one study which mentions the rate of increase in frequency in the occurrence of this symptom. Whittaker (212, *p. 475*) notes that, in his random sample of Standing Rock Sioux, 42% admitted experiencing blackouts, a quarter of whom reported "increasing frequency of occurrence." This statement is neither quantified nor correlated with quantity of intake preceding the symptom.

This symptom marks the end of the prodromal phase of alcohol addiction, which may have lasted anywhere from 6 months to 4 or 5 years, according to Jellinek (81, *p. 679*).

8. *Loss of Control [over drinking]:* INSUFFICIENT EVIDENCE

Jellinek (81, *pp. 679–680, 684*) considered this symptom the critical indicator of addictive drinking; its onset signals the beginning of the crucial or acute phase of alcohol addiction (Table 1 shows Jellinek's division of symptoms into phases). He described loss of control as follows (81, *pp. 679–680*):

> "*Loss of control (8)* means that any drinking of alcohol starts a chain reaction which is felt by the drinker as a physical demand for alcohol. This state, possibly a conversion phenomenon, may take hours or weeks for its full development; it lasts until the drinker is too intoxicated or too sick to ingest more alcohol.
> "The 'loss of control' is effective after the individual has started drinking, but it does not give rise to the beginning of a new drinking bout. The drinker has lost the ability to control the quantity once he has started, but he still can control whether he will drink on any given occasion or not. This is evidenced by the fact that after the onset of 'loss of control' the drinker can go through a period of voluntary abstinence ('going on the water wagon')."

Here Jellinek emphatically distinguished two different phenomena to be controlled: *(a)* the initiation of a bout; and *(b)* the quantity consumed once drinking begins, i.e., the duration of the bout. He offered no special descriptive phrase to cover the inability to control *(a)*; he called the inability to control *(b)* "loss of control."

In a later report by a World Health Organization committee (218), of which Jellinek was an influential member, *(a)* and *(b)* were distinguished from *(c)* steady drinking, a third, separate phenomenon to be controlled, which was designated the "inability to stop" drinking.

Thus, although Jellinek recognized three separate drinking phenomena which required control, he considered the inability to control only one of these as the critical diagnostic sign of alcohol addiction and reserved the term "loss of control" for it, i.e., *(b)* the quantity drunk and, hence, the duration of a bout.

Subsequently, Marconi (126) recognized two forms of "loss of control," suggested that they be distinguished from each other by separate terms, and supplied clarifying nomenclature: "inability to stop" for the inability to control *(b)* the quantity drunk and hence the duration of a bout (i.e., Jellinek's "loss of control"); and "inability to abstain" for the inability to refrain from *(c)* steady drinking (Jellinek's "inability to stop").

In effect, Marconi raised the concept of "loss of control" one level of generalization to serve as a cover term for the inability *(b)* to stop and *(c)* to abstain. It is not quite clear where the inability to refrain from *(a)* initiating a bout fits into Marconi's scheme.

Recently, Keller (94) has argued convincingly that although there do appear to be (at least) three separate phenomena which require control, the inability to control each of these is a manifestation of the same thing—the alcoholic's inability to consistently choose "whether he shall drink, and if he drinks . . . whether he shall stop" (94, *pp. 162, 163*). This inability, common to all three manifestations separately identified in the previous definitions, deserves the designation "loss of control."

It should be noted that in Keller's formulation the concept of "loss of control" has been raised one further level of abstraction beyond Marconi's usage, to serve as a cover term for the inability consistently to control each of the three phenomena separately identified in the earlier works.

Furthermore, Keller (94, *p. 159*) holds that *(c)* steady drinking is just an extreme form of *(a)* the inability to refrain from initiating a bout; both are examples of the same phenomenon—"inability to abstain." He says that if Marconi "had . . . gone one small step further . . . he must have made explicit . . . that the inability to abstain was really an inability to refrain—from starting!"

On the other hand, Keller (94, *p. 162*) considers the inability to control *(b)* the quantity consumed and hence the duration of a bout (Jellinek's "loss of control," Marconi and Keller's "inability to stop") as a secondary manifestation of loss of control, in the sense that it becomes activated by the inability to abstain in either of its two

CHART 1.—*Metamorphosis of the Term "Loss of Control"*

Author	a. Initiation of Bout	b. Quantity Drunk or Duration of Bout	c. Steady Drinking
Jellinek (81)	*	Loss of control	*
WHO (218)	*	Loss of control	Inability to stop
Marconi (126)	?	Inability to stop	Inability to abstain
		Loss of control	
Keller (94)	Inability to abstain	Inability to stop (a secondary phenomenon)	Inability to abstain
		Loss of control	

* It is inferred that the author recognized the "inability" as a separate phenomenon although he did not label it.

forms. Chart 1 summarizes this rather complicated metamorphosis of the loss-of-control concept from Jellinek to Keller.

Keller's reasoning centers on his belief that circumstances as well as individual characteristics determine the particular manifestation of loss of control which a specific person will exhibit. These circumstances are often culturally determined.

For example, in the U.S.A. social customs prevent most alcoholics from drinking during the working day. They "lack the opportunity, which they may dearly long for, to nibble between bouts" (94, *p. 163*). Except for the minority of addicts who no longer make any pretense of keeping a job, and perhaps housewives, social customs provide a partial substitute for individual control by limiting the manifestation of "loss of control" to the form of "inability to abstain," i.e., occasional bouts. On the other hand, in countries such as France, where custom does allow drinking during the working day, loss of control "enjoys" freer rein than in the U.S.A., and its most common manifestation is the form of "inability to abstain," i.e., the inability to refrain from *(c)* steady drinking (94, *p. 158*).

Once a bout begins, circumstances also determine the quantity consumed and hence the duration of a bout, i.e., the "secondary manifestation" of inability *(b)* to stop drinking.

Actually, rather than a separate phenomenon, Keller's inability *(b)* to stop a bout would seem better conceived as a continuum between *(a)* initiating a bout and *(c)* drinking steadily, day in and day out.

In other words, under Keller's formulation it seems appropriate to regard loss of control as a relative term. Recently, Bacon (4, *p. 4*) has been even more explicit on this point, emphasizing that "loss of control" is more process than "thing."

The duration of a bout is the yardstick of the degree of loss, which varies among individuals. In all cultures and subcultures, social customs reinforce to varying degrees whatever individual control is retained. The reinforcement is stronger over-all in some cultures than in others. Thus, the point on the continuum at which a particular person exercises control depends not only on the extent of his individual ability to do so, but on the degree to which his society's controls buttress his own. Similarly, the modal degree of manifestation of loss of control will vary among cultures.

Arguments about the meaning of "loss of control" are not mere semantic nitpicking. Jellinek (81, *p. 674*) and many others[19] have called loss of control the essence of alcohol addiction. Unfortunately, however, they have used the term to mean different things.

The practical implications of the choice among definitions are great. For example, Jellinek (81, *p. 674*) said that only those who exhibit "loss of control" suffer from the disease of alcohol addiction. Therefore, subjects who do not display this symptom conceivably could be denied treatment. Recent court cases—summarized by Fingarette (50)—have been decided on the issue of whether or not the defendant exhibited loss of control. The appropriateness of the decision obviously depends on the appropriateness of the definition of loss of control employed.

For example, if the meaning of loss of control were restricted to the inability to *(b)* interrupt a bout, following Jellinek (81) and some others, then the person who frequently or even occasionally can take a drink without starting a chain reaction to a drunken bout or steady drinking does not suffer from loss of control and hence is not an alcohol addict. Lately, we have been hearing more and more about such people.[20] If Jellinek's definition of loss of control is used, then

---

[19]E.g., Bacon (3, *p. 55*); Keller (91, *p. 313;* 94, *p. 153*); Lemere (106, *p. 204*); Cooperative Commission (26, *p. 39*); Ullman (197, *pp. 7, 8*); WHO (220).

[20]E.g., Davies (30); Mello et al. (132); Mello and Mendelson (133); Mendelson (134, *p. 21*); Mendelson et al. (135); Merry (136); Pattison (153, 154); Pattison et al. (155, *p. 624*) and nearly 20 studies cited therein; Robins et al. (163, *p. 402*); Sobell and Sobell (240); Tiebout et al. (189).

we must conclude either that they are not addicts, or that loss of control is not a necessary sign of alcohol addiction. Neither verdict seems to clarify alcohol addiction.

In any case, the question is how many times we have actually observed people who invariably go on a bender every time they take a drink. Keller (94, *p. 156*) says:

"Nearly all the alcoholics I have known . . . have told me that, even during the course of the severest stage of their active alcoholism, they had a drink or two or three on many occasions and stopped without further drinking, until on some other occasion, days or weeks later, they did not stop. Some could take a drink or two daily for days or weeks without going off on a bout."

If so, the question of how the doctrine that addicts can never drink normally became so widely accepted[21] is very much in order. Why is it even noteworthy that addicts can on occasion drink without initiating a bout?

Keller (94, *p. 154*) provides a plausible hypothesis to explain this anomaly, i.e., the great influence of Alcoholics Anonymous, and its slogan "one drink away from a drunk," on professionals in the alcohol field, including Jellinek. He does not deny, as others have done— e.g., Pattison et al. (155)—that the abstinence advocated by A.A. through this slogan is wise policy, at least for addicts of the A.A. type; but he does show that the "triggering effect" which underlies the slogan's doctrine of mandatory abstinence lacks scientific confirmation.

If we adopt Keller's broader definition of loss of control, many of these practical and theoretical dilemmas are avoided. For example, under Keller's formulation the alleged "paradox" of alcohol addicts without loss of control is revealed as more apparent than real. Behavior all the way from rare bouts (perhaps even interrupted by periods of controlled drinking) to steady drinking is considered a manifestation of loss of control, and hence a symptom of alcohol addiction, if the subject cannot consistently choose when such episodes will occur. The variation in frequency and duration of bouts reflects differences in the degree of control retained by the individual and exerted by his culture at a particular time.

Nevertheless, in case the arguments in favor of Keller's definition

[21]E.g., Jellinek (81, *p. 679*); Lemere (106, *p. 204*); Lester (109, *p. 429*); Marconi (126, *p. 219*); Pattison et al. (155, *p. 611*); Robins et al. (163, *pp. 402, 410*); Siegler et al. (173, *p. 587*).

do not seem compelling, the evidence which seems pertinent to the occurrence of this symptom among Indians is presented so as to enable separate consideration of evidence that applies to whichever of the definitions previously outlined may be preferred. That is, when it is fairly clear to which of Keller's three separate phenomena requiring control the observer intended an item of evidence to apply, it is discussed under that heading. The evidence in which this distinction is not easily drawn is presented separately. In addition, for reasons which will become clear later, the evidence has been divided into two additional categories which distinguish examples that merely suggest the subjects *do not* exercise control from those which more clearly indicate the subjects *cannot* control the phenomenon in question.

Examples of Absence of Control over Drinking

(a) Initiation of Bouts. It is clear that bouts are frequently initiated among the Indians covered in the literature. Many observers report the frequent occurrence of "binge,"[22] "spree,"[23] "splurge" (23, *p. 2*) or "blitz" (*27, pp. 121, 126*) drinking in the groups they report upon. In fact, most of these accounts suggest that the drinking style referred to by these terms is the predominant one among Indians. Although these labels are rarely explicitly defined (and may be only roughly synonymous), the descriptions of the episodes to which they refer suggest that all would qualify as references to "bouts," and demonstrate unequivocally that many of the Indians observed do not control the initiation of bouts.

Furthermore, it is frequently claimed that such bouts would be more common if Indians could afford frequent drinking.[24] Indeed, some studies indicate that liquor consumption (though not necessarily addiction or even problem drinking) increases directly with

[22]Clairmont (23, *p. 56*); Fahy and Muschenheim (40); Ferguson (46, *p. 2*; 48, *p. 901*); Freeman (52, *p. 158*); Hammer (58, *p. 290*); Keneally (97, *p. 3*); Kunitz et al. (101, *p. 682*); Levy and Kunitz (111, *p. 16*; 112, *p. 108*); Sanchez (168, *p. 2*); Whittaker (212, *p. 476*).

[23]Berreman (10, *p. 505*); Brody (16, *p. 11* ff.); Collins (25, *p. 115*); Geertz (230, *p. 99*); Honigmann (232, *p. 5*); Lemert (107, *pp. 322, 359*); Robbins (162, *p. 153*); Savard (169, *p. 911*); Szuter et al. (187, *p. 1*).

[24]Dailey (28, *p. 25*); Devereux (33, *p. 208*); Indian Affairs (225, *p. 3*); Lemert (108, *p. 104*); Slater (239, *p. 14*); Whittaker (212, *p. 475*).

economic success among Indians,[25] and a correlation between periodic receipts of cash and drinking sprees is often reported.[26]

(b) Quantity Consumed, Duration of a Bout. At first glance, loss of
control over the duration of a bout would seem to be inherent in the
binge drinking style documented above as prevalent among Indians.
Drinking parties are said to continue until the participants "pass
out,"[27] the supply is gone,[28] or some other exigency, such as lack of
funds or arrest,[29] interferes. Binges are said to last at least a full day,
and often for several days or even weeks.[30] Unfortunately, however,
few authors are as explicit as Whittaker (212, p. 476) in estimating
the frequency of individual bouts and the length of the intervening
period of abstinence, but a general picture of periodic,[31] prolonged
heavy drinking (Symptom 31) emerges.

These accounts strongly suggest that many Indians do not control
their alcohol intake once a bout begins.

Jellinek (81, p. 680) said that the addict tries to prove to himself
that he can drink like other people—that he has not lost control
over the quantity consumed and hence the duration of a bout. "To
'master his will' becomes a matter of greatest importance to him."
The evidence suggests this motivation may not be characteristic of
Indians. The reported prevalence of drinking with the express pur-

[25]E.g., Honigmann and Honigmann (69, p. 247; 70, pp. 80–81); Snyder
(178, p. 175); Whittaker (212, p. 473). However, Reifel (161, p. 6) says that
tavern business decreased as employment increased on the Sisseton reservation.

[26]E.g., Lemert (107, p. 323); Maynard (129, p. 40); Mindell (237, p. 6).

[27]Berreman (10, p. 507); Curley (27, p. 121); Dailey (28, p. 23); Devereux
(33, p. 226); Ferguson (47, p. 162); Hamer (58, p. 292; 59, p. 233); Heath
(62, p. 40); Kaplan and Johnson (89); Koolage (99, p. 102); Lemert
107, p. 310; 108, p. 96); Martinez (127, p. 3); Medicine (130, p. 10); Rohner
and Rohner (165, p. 47).

[28]Balikci (7, p. 196); Berreman (10, p. 506); Dailey (28, p. 23); Devereux
(33, p. 209); Hamer (58, p. 289); Hawthorn et al. (61, p. 12); Heath (62,
p. 38); Koolage (99, p. 97); Lemert (107, p. 310; 108, pp. 93, 96); Medicine
(130, p. 9); Robbins (162, p. 151); Rohner and Rohner (165, p. 47); Vachon
(203, p. 23).

[29]Hawthorn et al. (61, p. 12); Kuttner and Lorincz (103, p. 534); Medicine
(130, p. 9); Mindell (237, p. 6); Rohner and Rohner (165, p. 46).

[30]Berreman (10, p. 506); Du Toit (38, p. 19); Ferguson (46, p. 2; 48, p.
901); Hamer (58, p. 290); Hurt and Brown (74, p. 223); Koolage (99, p. 100);
Lemert (107, p. 322; 108, p. 93); Slotkin (175, p. 12); Whittaker (212, p. 476).

[31]Clairmont (23, p. 56); Hamer (59, p. 231); Honigmann and Honigmann
(233, p. 55); Horton (71, p. 240) [Maricopa, Papago]; Kunitz et al. (101,
p. 682); Lemert (108, p. 93); Slotkin (175, p. 12).

pose of getting drunk[32] suggests that Indians not only may feel no desire to prove they can master their will, but may even consciously seek the reverse. Whether or not this attitude reflects a value rooted in a traditional pursuit of ecstasy (29, *p. 57*), it puts loss of control in a new perspective.

(c) *Steady Drinking.* Steady drinking received considerable attention from Jellinek. He described it (84, *p. 38*) as the inability "to 'go on the water wagon' for even a day or two without the manifestation of withdrawal symptoms," and in elaborating it further he said: "Inveterate drinkers maintain a constant supply of alcohol in the blood at a level high enough to produce withdrawal symptoms when intake is stopped, but not necessarily at a level sufficient to produce intoxication."

Jellinek (84, *p. 38*) even designated steady drinking as a separate species (*delta*) of "alcoholism," as distinguished from other forms, including the one characterized by periodic bouts (*gamma*). He said the delta form is prevalent in some European countries, while gamma is the predominant form in the United States. However, Jellinek (81) did not include steady drinking as a separate item in his list of symptoms of alcohol addiction, probably because he considered it to be rare in the U.S.A. Nevertheless, he acknowledged (84, *p. 64*) that it does occur in this country.

Furthermore, the following description, included in his summary of the crucial phase of alcohol addiction, seems hard to distinguish from steady drinking (81, *p. 682*): "The first drink at rising, let us say at 7 A.M., is followed by another drink at 10 or 11 A.M., and another drink about 1 P.M., while the more intensive drinking hardly starts before 5 P.M." (However, Jellinek specifically cited the above behavior as an example of continual, i.e., recurring, in contrast to continuous, i.e., uninterrupted, drinking.) In any case, whether or not Jellinek recognized the steady drinking pattern as symptomatic of alcohol addiction, Keller's formulation establishes this behavior as a symptom of loss of control, and hence of alcohol addiction.

The occurrence of steady drinking among some Indians is specifically noted by a few authors. For example, Ferguson (48, *p. 902*) says of a Navaho sample: "The patients, like any other group of persons arrested for drunkenness, represented various types along a continuum from occasional destructive binge drinker to day-in day-

[32]Documented in footnote 3.

out inebriates showing signs of brain, liver or heart damage." Hawthorn et al. (61, *p. 12*) state that in British Columbia, "A few Indian reserves adjoin beer parlours, and here the drinking of some Indians is steady and almost daily, as long as money is available." Kuttner and Lorincz (103, *p. 534*) report that among the Indians of Omaha "The unemployed usually continued their drinking throughout the week," although it is not clear that this occurred all day long or even every day. Levy and Kunitz (113, *p. 232*) report that "The very high rate of death [from alcoholic cirrhosis] among the Hopi, a tribe even today noted for its sobriety and lack of public drinking, indicates the presence of a considerable amount of steady covert drinking." (Hence they make it clear that the occurrence of steady drinking was inferred from other evidence, rather than observed.) Elsewhere they (112, *p. 109*) also mention steady drinking among an unspecified portion of off-reservation Navaho with serious drinking problems.

The authors quoted above indicate that a few of the Indians they have observed do not refrain from steady drinking. On the other hand, three authors[33] make statements which might be construed as suggesting *(1)* that all the Indians in their sample do refrain from steady drinking and *(2)* that the observers rely heavily on this fact to support their opinion that alcohol addiction is rare in the observed group. Assuming that the latter inference was intended by these observers, it seems unjustified, because the pattern of steady drinking apparently is also rare in the dominant society, even among addicts. In any case, however, most observers of Indian drinking do not even address the question of the occurrence of steady drinking in their sample.

From the discussion above, it seems safe to conclude that some Indians in many of the groups covered exhibit absence of control over *(a)* initiation of bouts and *(b)* the duration of bouts. Absence of control over *(c)* steady drinking has not been firmly established; however, Keller's definition of loss of control allows, but does not require, the inclusion of the third phenomenon.

Nevertheless, Keller's criteria require demonstration of inability to control, rather than mere absence of control. The evidence presented so far may simply indicate unwillingness to control drinking. The problem is, as MacAndrew (120, *p. 497*) points out, that "the

---

[33]Berreman (10, *p. 511*); Devereux (33, *p. 209*); Lemert (107, *p. 362*).

existence of this 'loss of control' cannot be independently determined but must be inferred on the basis of the failure of the chronic drunkard to comport himself in the manner of a prudent man." Even in the dominant society, standards of prudence vary in different segments of the population, and thus it is not always certain that a person who does not control his drinking in accordance with a particular standard actually cannot do so.

In a subculture such as that of Indians, standards of "prudence" may be quite different from those of any other segment of the population. In fact, I think later discussions will clearly demonstrate that they are. Therefore, in this group the inference of loss of control from evidence of its absence is particularly tenuous.

Furthermore, standards of prudence are not the only pertinent cultural variable. For example, as suggested earlier, Indians might drink a lot more than they do if they could afford it. In circumstances where people are absolutely unable to finance a bout, abstinence is hardly a fair measure of the extent of their control over drinking.

Thus, even if we had firm data on the proportion of Indians and, for comparison, of dominant-society members who do not control their drinking, such evidence would merely indicate the relative incidence of absence of control rather than inability to control such behavior; but only the latter is pertinent to our attempt to determine the comparative rates of loss of control, and hence of alcohol addiction, in the two groups.

Evidence of Inability to Control Drinking

The literature does contain a few statements[34] which suggest that the individuals reported upon were unable rather than simply unwilling to control their drinking. That is, the authors make it clear that loss of control has not been inferred from mere failure to exercise control, but from observations of people who had tried, to no avail, to control their drinking. Most of these accounts are rather vaguely phrased in terms of unsuccessful attempts to "stop drinking"; but a few refer rather clearly to a desire to control one or more of the three manifestations of loss of control distinguished by Keller (94).

Berreman (10, *p. 511*) says of some Nikolski natives: "Two or three

[34]Berreman (10, *p. 511*); Heath (62, *p. 53*); Lemert (107, *p. 367*); Rohner and Rohner (165, *p. 48*); Savard (169, *p. 913*); Szuter et al. (187, *p. 2*); Slater (239, *pp. 9, 15, 19*); Werner (209, *p. 3*).

other villagers have decided to quit drinking at times, but these re-
solves have been short-lived. Most people simply have no reason
or desire to stop and there are no social pressures for them to do so."

Ferguson (48, *p. 907*) reports that 79% of a population of Navaho
heavy drinkers admitted they were unable to quit after one or two
drinks, i.e., to control (*b*) the duration of a bout. One of Heath's
(62, *p. 53*) Navaho informants stated, "I tried to stop [drinking]
once but couldn't. Besides, anybody in my job [driver of a school
bus] needs a drink once in a while." Lemert (107, *p. 367*) reports
"weakly motivated attempts to stop drinking" among some Northwest Coast Indians. Mindell (237, *p. 3*) says a group of drinkers
referred to a Pine Ridge treatment program from the jail seemed to
be "weighted toward . . . the chronic alcoholic. This person has been
drinking a long time—many months to years, steadily, wants to get
off alcohol at times but can't manage it." Rohner and Rohner (165,
p. 48) say that "occasionally some of the [Kwakiutl] villagers became
concerned about drinking too much." Savard (169, *p. 913*) claims
that "The alcoholics [at Fort Defiance Hospital] reported growing
weary at times of the high cost in physical pain and social dysfunc-
tioning of the benefits they derived from alcohol and they tried to
abstain. But any attempt to refuse a drink from a member of the
fellowship was countered by a concerted, unrelenting pressure to
drink." Referring to the same group, Szuter et al. (185, *p. 2*) say,
"patients presented themselves . . . on a purely volunteer basis. Many
indicated a desire to stop drinking which, in spite of repeated attempts, they had been unable to do on their own."

In Slater's Uintah-Ouray sample (239, *p. 9*), "53% indicated they
wanted to stop [drinking] but they didn't know how." In addition,
33% reported they had looked for help with their drinking problem
(239, *p. 19*). In Whittaker's (212, *pp. 475–476*) sample of Standing
Rock Sioux, 45% reported they had felt like having a drink whether
they wanted to or not—"like they couldn't help themselves." In addition, 76% had set a limit to the amount they planned to drink, but 46%
reported they were rarely able to hold the limit; that is, they couldn't
control (*b*) the duration of a bout.

Although the statements quoted above sound suspiciously like
references to manifestations of loss of control over drinking in Keller's sense, i.e., inability to control, this evidence does not meet the
criteria used herein for positively rating the occurrence of a symptom
of alcohol addiction. The number of statements—10—is less than

half the average number cited in justification of ratings. (One symptom is later rated PRESENT on the basis of only 8 statements but among these is an authoritative source that claims the symptom frequently occurs among Indian groups throughout the country.) As the basis for subsequent definite symptom ratings is described, I think it will be obvious that the evidence concerning loss of control does not measure up. Therefore, this critical diagnostic sign of alcohol addiction is rated INSUFFICIENT EVIDENCE.

However, even if we had firm evidence of inability to control drinking among Indians, a further semantic problem must be addressed. Keller equated loss of control with inability to control drinking, which seems to imply that everyone who exhibits inability to control drinking started out with the ability but lost it. In a recent elaboration of social aspects of loss of control, Bacon (4, *p. 8*) makes this explicit:

"It is axiomatic that control has to be present before it can be lost. If an individual never had control (and this is quite possible) or had adopted a set of controls different from and incompatible with those of the dominant group, then he or she might become a great problem to others but not because of a loss of control."

If Bacon means to imply that the label alcohol addict is appropriately applied only to people who suffer from *loss* of control in its literal sense, this seems pertinent to our attempt to determine whether any Indians qualify as addicts.

Since very few North American Indian groups had alcohol aboriginally (118, *p. 392*), one might claim that they had no controls, individual or social, over the substance. Furthermore, although Indian groups have had at least (depending on the time of White contact) 100 years in which to develop such controls, circumstances have militated against this. As Stewart (184, *p. 66*) says:

"Indians alone have been subjected to selective prohibition against use of alcohol for over a century and a half. From the passage of the general Indian Intercourse Act of 1832 until 1953, it was illegal nationally for Indians to possess liquor in any form anyplace. Since 1953, most tribal councils, some states (i.e., Utah) and some local communities have continued to try to limit Indian drinking by law. Indians never had the opportunity to learn the proper everyday, family, self-regulated use of alcoholic beverages."

Therefore, if controls over drinking are culturally determined, and if Indians have never socially or culturally internalized such controls, we might be tempted to conclude that their absence in the group should not be interpreted as *loss* of control, i.e., a symptom of alcohol addiction. Under such circumstances, Keller[35] is willing to entertain the notion that perhaps "conceptions of loss of control in Jellinek's and Keller's sense simply do not apply. If so, loss of control cannot be for Indians the pathognomonic diagnostic sign of addiction to alcohol. One would have to look for other signs."

But perhaps this is going too far. For one thing, some Indians do control their drinking in accordance with dominant-society standards. These Indians are by no means restricted to groups which had alcohol aboriginally; on the contrary, in one group which did have alcohol before White contact, i.e., the Western Apache, Levy and Kunitz (111, *p. 17*) have inferred that "excessive alcohol consumption is not a negligible problem," which suggests that controls over drinking may be weak or absent.

Furthermore, it seems likely that some who previously drank in a "controlled" fashion no longer do so, and perhaps are even included among those reported earlier as unable to control their drinking. Surely these have *lost* control over drinking in Keller's terms. To argue that Indians have not lost control over drinking because they never learned it in the first place, and hence cannot be diagnosed as alcohol addicts on the basis of absence of control, seems oversimplistic in many ways.

On the other hand, the other circumstance identified by Bacon (4), in which loss of control would be a dubious criterion of alcohol addiction, may well be applicable in the case of Indians. That is, they may have "adopted a set of controls different from and incompatible with those of the dominant group." Later discussions will suggest this may be the case among Indians.

The foregoing lengthy discussion seemed necessary because loss of control over drinking is considered the single most important criterion of alcohol addiction, and yet, unfortunately, it appears to be one of the most elusive to apply. Even in the dominant society the occurrence of the symptom often must be indirectly inferred. In subcultures, such as Indian groups, the problems of identifying and interpreting the significance of the occurrence or nonoccurrence of loss of control seem extremely complex, and deserve detailed study.

We are not specifically concerned with what *type* of alcohol addiction occurs among Indians. If we can determine whether addiction

[35]Keller, M. Personal communication, 27 February 1973.

of any type occurs in this group, the objective here will have been met. However, this is a convenient place to refer to some attempts to fit Indian drinking into Jellinek's (84, 85) species of alcoholism.

In addition to two types of addictive alcoholism, i.e., *gamma* (bout drinking) and *delta* (steady drinking), Jellinek (85) recognized a species designated *epsilon*. He considered this type to be insufficiently known to describe in detail. He said it was characterized by periodic explosive drinking; this adjective suggests that the behavior would perhaps differ from gamma in degree. However, he did not indicate whether he considered it to be addictive or not (*alpha* and *beta*, the two other types, were specifically labeled nonaddictive).

At first glance, this brief reference to *epsilon* sounds as though it might be pertinent to Indian drinking, which certainly seems "explosive" in most of the accounts cited so far. However, Dailey (28, *p. 26*), who worked with Jellinek when the latter was research director at the Addiction Research Foundation in Toronto, says:

"If one adopts Jellinek's classifications, the Indians' excessive use of alcohol does cause damage (mostly social and economic) and may, therefore, be identified as an instance of 'alcoholism.' I would quickly add, however, that the species is not any of those familiar to us such as *Alpha, Beta, Delta* or *Gamma*. Rather it might be called *Zeta*—a unique pattern of use in which drinking is periodic and explosive, but nonaddictive."

Elaborating further on this theme, Dailey says:[36]

"With respect to the question of Jellinek's patterns, I introduced the idea of *Zeta* because I did not think that Indian drinking which is explosive but not addictive . . . fit the *Epsilon* species. I might add that while I was associated with the Foundation in Ontario, it was the opinion of our research director that Indian drinking was of a different species than those defined by Jellinek."

Jellinek (84, 85) had not in fact claimed that his list of species was exhaustive. It may well be that Indian drinking is sufficiently unique to qualify as a separate species, which might or might not be addictive.

However, it should be pointed out that Keller's (94) definition of loss of control seems to upset Jellinek's (84, 85) whole scheme of "species" of alcoholism. For example, it seems to eliminate the basis for distinguishing *delta* (steady drinking) from *gamma* (bout drinking) alcoholism. The other changes in Jellinek's scheme which would

[36]Dailey, R. C. Personal communication, 8 July 1971.

follow logically from Keller's modifications of the loss-of-control concept would require a more detailed discussion than can be accommodated here.

9. Rationalize Drinking Behavior: INSUFFICIENT EVIDENCE

Jellinek (81, *p. 680*) describes this symptom as follows:

"[The addict] produces the well-known alcoholic 'alibis.' He finds explanations which convince him that he did not lose control, but that he had a good reason to get intoxicated and that in the absence of such reasons he is able to handle alcohol as well as anybody else. These rationalizations are needed primarily for himself and only secondarily for his family and associates. The rationalizations make it possible for him to continue with his drinking, and this is of the greatest importance to him as he knows no alternative for handling his problems."

According to the literature on Indian alcohol use, the reasons for drinking most frequently offered by informants run heavily to forthright statements such as "to have fun," "to celebrate," "for kicks," or "to feel good."[37] Rationalizations such as "because my wife nags me," which are familiar in the dominant society, seem to be relatively rare in the Indian groups covered herein. For example, in literature on the Navaho, Heath (62, *p. 24*) encountered only two instances of apparent rationalizations for drinking behavior. In another case (Northwest Coast) Lemert (107, *p. 366*) reported that rationalizations were not offered as an excuse by the drinker, but rather by his friends or family.

On the other hand, as in the case of guilt feelings, the relative absence of this symptom may have been exaggerated. In Whittaker's (213, *p. 81*) Standing Rock Sioux sample, 25% offered no reasons for drinking; thus 75% felt compelled to offer some explanation, at least to the interviewer. Several works cite statements by members of various Indian groups which could be interpreted as rationalizations of their drinking behavior. These include: invocation of the firewater myth that Indians just can't handle liquor;[38] diffusion—Indians learned problem drinking from the White man (165, *p. 46*); pressure to drink from family or companions;[39] witchcraft (48, *pp. 907, 911*);

[37]Berreman (10, *pp. 505, 509*); Boyce (13, *p. 26*); Clairmont (22, *p. 9; 23, p. 61*); Heath (63, *pp. 127, 132*); Honigmann and Honigmann (68, *p. 589; 69, p. 200; 70, pp. 73, 78*); Lemert (107, *p. 336*); Medicine (130, *p. 10*); Mindell (237, *pp. 4, 6*); Robbins (162, *p. 158*); Slater (238, *p. 3; 239, p. 7*).

[38]See Chapter 1, footnote 3.

[39]Berreman (10, *p. 509*); Graves (57, *p. 48*); Hurt and Brown (74, *p. 229*); Littman (117, *p. 1777*); Mindell (237, *p. 6*); Slater (239, *p. 8*).

boredom or "nothing else to do";[40] and various "personal effects"[41] reasons, including "false courage",[42] to avoid being called a sissy (13, p. 26), to forget worries or sorrow,[43] release,[44] deprivation (economic, cultural, spiritual),[45] and a variety of other reasons of this type.[46]

Seldom is it clear, however, whether these "rationalizations" are offered to the outside observer only, or to other Indians. Only the latter would conform to the spirit of Jellinek's description of the symptom. Furthermore, the same "rationalizations" figure prominently among the "causes" of the high incidence of problem drinking among Indians postulated by experts.[47] One man's "rationalization" may be another man's fact. Therefore, pending more direct evidence on this question, it seems prudent to avoid interpreting the reasons

[40]Berreman (10, p. 509); Boyce (13, p. 26); Heath (63, p. 132); Lemert (107, p. 336); Littman (116, p. 70); Slater (238, pp. 3, 14; 239, pp. 8, 9).

[41]For descriptions of "personal effects" drinking see Jessor et al. (87, pp. 170–175) and Mulford and Miller (142). This category seems to be similar to Fallding's "facilitative drinking" (41, p. 719), Whittaker's "individual" drinking" (213, p. 81), Bales' "utilitarian drinking" (6, p. 487), which the latter considered the type most likely to lead to compulsive drinking (6, p. 496).

[42]Boyce (13, p. 26); Martinez (127, p. 6); Medicine (130, p. 18).

[43]Berreman (10, p. 509); Boyce (13, p. 26); Medicine (130, p. 10).

[44]Hamer (58, p. 286); Lemert (107, p. 322); Littman (116, p. 70); Robbins (162, p. 131).

[45]American Indian Workshop (222, p. 3); Lemert (107, p. 337); Medicine (130, p. 10); Slater (238, p. 3).

[46]Berreman (10, p. 509); Jessor et al. (87, p. 179); Lemert (107, p. 337); Littman (116, p. 71); Martinez (127, p. 6); Savard (169, p. 912); Slater (239, p. 10).

[47]For a few examples see the following: Fulfill drunken Indian stereotype: Dozier (36, p. 85); Honigmann and Honigmann (70, p. 78); Hurt and Brown (74, p. 229); Lemert (107, p. 335); Littman (117, p. 1777); Whittaker (213, p. 84). Diffusion: Berreman (10, p. 505); Frederickson (51, p. 13); Honigmann (232, p. 5); Honigmann and Honigmann (70, p. 78); Lemert (108, p. 97); MacAndrew and Edgerton (121, pp. 136 ff.). Pressure to drink from family or friends: see Symptom 10. Nothing else to do: American Indian Workshop (222, p. 3); Berreman (10, p. 511); Curley (27, pp. 129, 130); Dailey (28, p. 25); Dozier (36, p. 85); Du Toit (38, p. 19); Ferguson (47, p. 160); Hamer (58, pp. 292, 294); Honigmann and Honigmann (70, p. 78), but see (69, p. 200); Hurt (73, p. 228); Hurt and Brown (74, p. 229); Indian Affairs (225, p. 3); Lemert (107, p. 335, 108, p. 96); Littman (117, p. 1777); Mindell (237, p. 6); Szuter et al. (187, p. 4); Whittaker (213, p. 84). Some "personal effects" reasons are postulated by almost every work addressing the question of why problem drinking is so common among Indians.

offered by Indians for their drinking as rationalizations in Jellinek's sense.

As in the case of several other symptoms, it might be possible to infer the absence of this symptom from the apparent absence of guilt feelings (Symptom 5), but I reject this alternative for the reasons set forth in the discussion of Symptom 6.

10. Social Pressures (Countered): ABSENT–RARE

Jellinek (81, p. 680) says that while an addict's system of rationalization originates largely from inner needs, it also serves to counter social pressures, which arise at the time of loss of control when drinking behavior becomes conspicuous and those around him begin to reprove the alcoholic.

Many students of Indian drinking claim that in the groups they describe problem drinkers are not reproved; thus there would appear to be little social pressure against drinking to be countered.[48] The literature indicates that in most of the groups covered herein drunkenness is considered an adequate excuse for behavior which otherwise would be condemned[49], and hence, problem drinkers are not rejected.[50]

[48]Berreman (10, p. 511); Boyce (13, p. 20); Boyer (14, pp. 219, 232); Chance (21, p. 66); Clairmont (22, p. 11); Collins (25, p. 122); Curley (27, pp. 125, 129); Dailey (28, p. 25); Du Toit (38, p. 18); Ferguson (46, p. 2; 47, p. 163; 48, p. 902); Graves (56, p. 318); Hamer (58, p. 294); Heath (62, pp. 25, 47, 68); Honigmann and Honigmann (68, p. 615; 233, pp. 50–52); Hurt and Brown (74, pp. 223, 230); IHS Task Force (75, p. 3) quoting Wissler (217); Jessor (86, p. 72); Jessor et al. (87, p. 265); Kaplan and Johnson (89, p. 220); Lemert (107, pp. 356, 365; 108, pp. 101–103); Levy (110, p. 317); Littman (116, p. 74; 117, p. 1770), and citing Bollinger and Starkey (227); McKinley (123, p. 32); Maynard (129, pp. 39, 49); Medicine (130, pp. 4, 18); Rohner and Rohner (165, pp. 46, 50); Sanchez (168, p. 3); Savard (169, p. 912); Southwest Indian Alcoholism Council (179, p. 7); Whittaker (213, pp. 84, 85).

[49]Belmont (9, p. 63); Berreman (10, pp. 507, 508); Boyer (14, pp. 218, 219, 231, 270); Carpenter (19, p. 151); Clairmont (22, p. 11; 23, p. 64); Curley (27, pp. 121, 122); Dailey (28, pp. 23, 26; 29, pp. 55–56); Devereux (33, p. 213); Hamer (58, pp. 287, 293; 59, p. 238); Heath (62, pp. 25, 53, 79); Hurt and Brown (74, pp. 223, 229); IHS Task Force (75, p. 14); Koolage (99, pp. 101, 158); Lemert (107, p. 366; 108, p. 103); Littman (116, p. 70); Maynard (129, pp. 39, 49); Robbins (162, p. 153); Sanchez (168, p. 1); Slater (239, p. 21); Slotkin (175, p. 12).

[50]Boyer (14, p. 213); Curley (27, p. 129); Devereux (33, p. 211); Ferguson (47, p. 163); Hamer (58, p. 293); Honigmann and Honigmann (68, pp. 591, 595); Kuttner and Lorincz (103, p. 539); Lemert (107, pp. 356, 364; 108,

On the contrary, pressure to drink appears to be extremely strong in a majority of the groups covered.[51] An etiquette of sharing[52] may play a double role in promoting problem drinking among Indians. In addition to discouraging refusal of drinks, sharing could preclude the accumulation of property. Some observers have suggested that the resultant frustrations could lead to problem drinking among acculturating Indians.[53]

The Hopi seem to provide one striking exception to the norm of weak social sanctions depicted in the literature. For example, Kunitz et al. (102, p. 717) say the Hopi condemn drinking and impose sanctions against it: "The 'Hopi way' has valued harmony and peace and eschewed 'acting out.' In addition, the traditional method of social control among the Hopi has involved a reliance on gossip, witchcraft accusations, and ultimate ejection from the community." The Hopi, at least those from traditional villages, may also practice geographical escape (see Symptom 22) in anticipation of ejection, which would seem to qualify as a form of "countering social pressure" against drinking.

The high incidence of both problem drinking and weak social sanctions against drinking in most of the Indian groups suggests

p. 101); Littman (116, p. 73); Maynard (129, p. 35); Robbins (162, p. 159); Savard (169, p. 912); Whittaker (213, p. 86).

[51]American Indian workshop (222, p. 1, 3); Boyce (13, p. 26); Clairmont (22, p. 9; 23, p. 61); Collins (25, pp. 113, 127); Ferguson (47, p. 163; 48, p. 917); Graves (57, p. 48); Heath (62, p. 23; 63, p. 125); Honigmann and Honigmann (68, p. 590); Hurt and Brown (74, p. 229); IHS Task Force (75, p. 14); Koolage (99, p. 101); Lemert (107, pp. 310, 372, 388; 108, pp. 93, 104); Littman (116, p. 72; 117, p. 1777); Manning (125, p. 7); Maynard (129, p. 39); Medicine (130, p. 9); Mindell (237, p. 5); Robbins (162, p. 158); Savard (169, p. 913-914); Slater (238, p. 3; 239, p. 18); Spang (180, p. 29); Szuter et al. (187, p. 4); Tax, quoted in Geyer (54). A few observers offer evidence or opinion that indicates pressure to drink may have been overestimated, i.e., Devereux (33, p. 211); Slater (239, pp. 11-19); Whittaker (213, p. 86).

[52]Balikci (7, p. 196); Dailey (28, pp. 23, 25, 26); Devereux (33, pp. 209, 240); Ferguson (47, p. 162; 48, p. 901); Heath (62, p. 37; 63, p. 125); Honigmann and Honigmann (68, p. 589; 234, p. 21); Hurt and Brown (74, pp. 222, 224); IHS Task Force (75, pp. 8, 14); Koolage (99, pp. 103, 105); Kuttner and Lorincz (103, pp. 533, 534); Lemert (107, p. 307); Medicine (130, p. 9); Mindell (237, p. 6); Reifel (161, p. 5); Robbins (162, pp. 86, 158); Rohner and Rohner (165, p. 46); Sanchez (168, p. 1); Swett (241, p. 12); Whittaker (213, p. 86).

[53]Indian Affairs (225, p. 4); Reifel (161, p. 5); Spindler and Spindler (181, p. 151).

that stronger pressures might serve as a deterrent. Some Hopi seem to belie this view. As will be seen later (Symptom 27), they exhibit an exceptionally high rate of alcoholic cirrhosis. Apparently the social pressures applied by the traditional segments of the group simply drive problem drinkers into solitary clandestine drinking[54] or away from the Indian community into border towns (101, *p. 683*) where heavy drinking continues.

Adherents of Christian sects and Peyotists provide exceptions to the rule of weak social sanctions against drinking in American Indian groups (1, *p. 188*).

The literature includes a few more indications of mild forms of social pressure against drinking, particularly from wives (e.g., 25, *p. 122; 57, pp. 40, 41, 49*). The title "There But for Grace" (57, *p. 53*) suggests that this phenomenon is a prominent theme in a manuscript on Denver Navaho currently in preparation by T. D. Graves.

But on balance the literature depicts social pressures against drinking as very mild in all groups except some Hopi. For the symptom rating in Table 2, I have combined the statements about *(a)* the absence of social pressure against drinking, *(b)* use of drunkenness as an excuse for otherwise unacceptable behavior and *(c)* the lack of rejection of problem drinkers.[55] Together these yield 34 "accounts" covering modern groups in 8 culture areas, plus 1 miscellaneous group and 3 generalizations about American Indians. All 3 community types appear in the list (cf. Appendix).

From the apparent rarity of social pressures against drinking, as indicated in these statements, I have inferred that the symptom "social pressures (countered)" would be equally rare in these groups.

11. Grandiose Behavior: INSUFFICIENT EVIDENCE

Display of grandiosity is one way to compensate for the marked loss of self-esteem which the alcohol addict is said to experience (81, *p. 680*): "Extravagant expenditures and grandiloquence convince him that he is not as bad as he had thought at times."

---

[54]See Symptoms 16A, and Kunitz et al. (102, *p. 717*) and Levy and Kunitz (112, *p. 117*).

[55]Footnotes 48, 49 and 50 contain 46 pertinent citations. Of these, 34 qualify as "accounts": (10), (13), (14), (21), (22 and 23), (25), (27), (28), (33), (38), (46, 47 and 48), (56), (58 and 59), (62), (68 and 233), (74), (86 and 87), (89), (99), (103), (107 and 108), (110), (116 and 117), (123), (129), (130), (162), (165), (168), (169), (175), (179), (213), (239).

Many of the statements cited earlier to document the etiquette of sharing in a number of Indian groups[56] indicate that many Indians spend a great deal of money offering drinks to their friends—probably more than would be considered prudent in the dominant society. But the desire for esteem which this behavior reflects seems in no way unique to the problem drinker in Indian groups. Drink sharing is depicted as the norm even for occasional drinkers. The etiquette of sharing possessions, including liquor, could account for whatever element of "grandiose behavior" offering drinks might be interpreted to reflect, without recourse to alcohol addiction as an explanation.

Most of the accounts of drinking behavior which might be interpreted as "grandiose" seem to be correlated with various traditional behaviors in the observed groups. For example, boasting of exploits and cultural sanctioning of recklessness among Apache (52, *p. 198*) and the Dakota (74, *p. 223*); temporary assumption of make-believe status positions of prestige, involving bragging and exaggeration among the Potawatomi (59, *pp. 235-236*); and older patterns of competition and rivalry among the Northwest Coast Indians (107, *p. 324*) and the Naskapi (162, *p. 165*). In cases where grandiose behavior may have roots in traditional norms, alcohol addiction is not necessarily indicated by its presence, even in association with alcohol.

The remaining reports of behavior which might fit the pattern described as "grandiose" by Jellinek are not accompanied by any suggestion of a tie to traditional behavior. In fact, these accounts concern groups in which grandiose behavior would seem to be foreign to traditional norms—for example, the Navaho (62, *p. 51;* 89) and the Salmon Indians (68, *p. 594*). However, these reports cover too few groups to justify rating "grandiose behavior" as present among Indians as a whole.

Some authors, e.g., Lemert (108, *p. 93*), have described noteworthy qualitative changes in behavior among Indians when they drink; others, e.g., Devereux (33, *p. 215*), say the changes seem to be quantitative only. (Additional examples of conflicting views on behavioral changes brought on by alcohol among Indians are presented in the discussion of the next symptom, "marked aggressive behavior.") Disagreement on this subject might reflect actual behavioral differences among groups, or might result from the ac-

[56]See footnote 52.

cident of what has been observed. Heath (62, *p. 45*) notes that the effects of drinking are markedly variable among the Navaho. This seems to be true also in the dominant society, as observation at any cocktail party reveals. Perhaps intoxicated behavior is highly variable among and within individuals in all alcohol-using groups.

The evidence provided in the literature thus far is insufficient to justify rating "grandiose behavior." Even if such behavior did occur at a relatively high rate among Indians, it might not be a reliable indicator of the occurrence of alcohol addiction in groups where such behavior seems to have traditional roots.

12. Marked Aggressive Behavior: CONFLICTING EVIDENCE

Jellinek (81, *p. 680*) notes that marked aggressive behavior is the first sign of a "system of isolation" which has its roots in an alcohol addict's system of rationalization: "The rationalizations quite naturally lead to the idea that the fault lies not within himself, but in others, and thus results in a progressive withdrawal from the social environment. The first sign of this attitude is a marked aggressive behavior."

If Jellinek meant that isolation and rationalizations are necessary preconditions for the development of the symptom "marked aggressive behavior" under the influence of alcohol, it is ironic that a stereotype of drunken violence (one of the firewater-myth motifs) should have been applied to a group in which the occurrence of the "preconditions" for such behavior is not firmly established.[57]

Modern accounts of Indian drinking, however, do suggest that it is likely to lead to aggressive acts in the groups reported upon.[58] A few observers point out that drunken aggressive acts are most

[57]See, for example, ratings in Table I and discussion of Symptoms 5, 9, 10, 13, 16, 16A, 19, 20, 22 and 35.

[58]Andre (226, *p. 5*); Baker (5, *p. 270*); Boyer (14, *p. 217*); Clark (24, *pp. 5, 6*); Collins (25, *p. 127*); Curley (27, *p. 121*); Dailey (28, *pp. 22, 26*); Du Toit (38, *p. 19*); Geertz (230, *p. 99*); Hamer (59, *pp. 233, 237*); Heath (62, *p. 46; 63, pp. 126, 131*); von Hentig (66, *p. 80*); Honigmann and Honigmann (70, *p. 75* for preadministrative controls; and 69, *p. 201*); Hurt and Brown (74, *pp. 223, 230*); Jessor (86, *p. 69*); Kaplan and Johnson (89, *pp. 216 et seq.*); Koolage (99, *pp. 100, 102*); Kuttner and Lorincz (103, *p. 539*); Lemert (107, *pp. 342 et seq.; 108, p. 94*); Littman (116, *p. 70*); Robbins (162, *p. 165*); Rohner and Rohner (165, *p. 50*); Slotkin (175, *p. 12*); Spindler and Spindler (181, *p. 155*); Stewart (184, *pp. 63–64*); Whittaker (213, *p. 83*), and quoting Kaplan (235).

often committed by particular segments of an Indian population, e.g., the "young (74, *p. 223;* 108, *p. 94*) or the "poor" (25, *p. 127*), but in most other accounts the generalizations seem to apply to the group as a whole. Seldom is it clear, however, whether the observer considers the incidence of alcohol-related aggression to be higher among Indians than in the general population.

MacAndrew and Edgerton (121, *pp. 100–164*) provide historical and modern documentation of exceptions to the "rule" that when Indians get drunk their comportment is characterized by "horrendous changes-for-the-worse" (*p. 101*).

A number of other authors have remarked on the comparative lack of overt drunken aggression in the groups they observed. For example, Balikci (7, *p. 197*) says that among the Vunta Kutchin feelings of hostility and repulsion "are so prevalent as to form a social pattern . . . yet predispositions to engage in overt conflict are considerably less frequent. Violent quarrels and fights do occur, mostly under the influence of alcohol, but only a very few of the covert hostile relations explode in violence and openly conflictual interaction." Berreman (10, *p. 507*) says that "although some individuals have reputations for becoming aggressive or nasty when drunk . . . fights or other physical violence are uncommon" in the Aleut group he studied. Devereux (33, *p. 216*) remarks on the rarity of drunken brawls and of drunken aggression among the Mohave. Hawthorn et al. (61, *p. 13*) suggest that newspapers tend to exaggerate instances of death or physical damage as a result of intoxication among Indians in British Columbia by ignoring similar events among Whites while systematically reporting the incidents among Indians.

According to several observers, the notion that Indians would be relatively peaceful citizens, but for the demon drink, is common folklore in both the Indian[59] and surrounding White[60] communities they have studied. A few authors apparently accept as fact the notion

[59]E.g., Brody (16, *p. 48*); Clairmont (22, *p. 11, 23, p. 64*); Honigmann and Honigmann (70, *p. 79*); Swett (241, *p. 19*).

[60]Balikci (7, *p. 195*); Clairmont (22, *p. 11; 23, p. 64*); Heath (63, *p. 131*); Henderson (64, *p. 8*); Honigmann and Honigmann (69, *pp. 154, 197;* 70, *p. 75*); Indian Affairs (225, *p. 3*); Jicarilla Apache Alcoholism Project (88, p. 75); Lemert (107, *pp. 345, 356*); Levy et al. (115, *p. 129*); Levy and Kunitz (111, *p. 16*); Martinez (127, *p. 5*); Maynard (129, *p. 47*); Savard (169, *p. 910*); Slater (238, *p. 7*).

that most Indian aggression is associated with alcohol,[61] but it is sometimes explicitly questioned or denied.[62] In the case of Navaho homicide, for example, Levy et al. (115, *p. 146*) report: "We were unable to demonstrate any association, positive or negative, between the act of homicide and the use of alcohol." Kuttner and Lorincz (103, *p. 539*), who are not proponents of the reverse-firewater hypothesis, comment wryly:

"White men are aggressive both while drunk and sober, and assault not only wives and other relatives, but also total strangers; yet reservoirs of hostility are not included in the anthropological description of the White man. If aggression is revealed by the Indian only when he is intoxicated, then his control over his emotions is superior to that of the White man when he is sober. Why persons with better stability should be more prone to alcoholism remains unanswered."

The notion that Indians are unusually aggressive when drinking is most often based on arrest statistics. The use of arrest rates as indicators of relative aggression rates among Indians is open to challenge on a number of grounds.

If differential enforcement is practiced, arrest rates would not provide a reliable indication of the relative rates of commission of the offenses in question by members of the two groups. Some observers[63] suggest that Indians are more likely to be arrested for a given offense than Whites. For example, Indian drinking appears to be more public than White drinking,[64] and thus involves higher exposure to arrest, even if rates of drinking were the same or lower. On the other hand, other observers[65] express the opinion that White

[61]Andre (226, *p. 5*); Baker (5, *p. 270*); Balikci (7, *p. 195*); Du Toit (38, *p. 20*); Ferguson (47, *p. 162*) citing Young (221); Hamer (58, *p. 293; 59, p. 239*); Hawthorn et al. (61, *p. 13a*); Heath (62, *p. 9; 63, p. 121*) citing Van Valkenburgh (204, *pp. 53–54*) [homicide]; Henderson (64, *p. 8*) citing Young (221); Horton (71, *p. 252*) [Naskapi and others]; Hurt and Brown (74, *pp. 224, 228*) [arrests]; Indian Affairs (225, *p. 3*); Lemert (107, *p. 341; 108, pp. 95–96*); Martinez (127, *p. 5*); Maynard (129, *p. 39*); Rohner and Rohner (165, *p. 51*); Sanchez (168, *p. 2*); Stewart (184, *pp. 63–64*); Suarez (185, *p. 1192*); White (211, *p. 153*); Whittaker (213, *p. 83*).

[62]Berreman (10, *p. 507*); Brody (16, *p. 35*); Devereux (33, *pp. 210, 216*); Honigmann and Honigmann (68, *p. 592; 234, p. 21*); Levy et al. (115, *p. 146*); Littman (116, *p. 71*); Slater (239, *p. 19*).

[63]For example, as suggested by Clairmont (22, *p. 10*); Heath (62, *p. 47*); and Levy and Kunitz (113, *p. 226*).

[64]See footnote 7.

[65]For example, as suggested by Boyer (14, *p. 218*) and Lemert (107, *p. 356; 108, pp. 102–103*).

and Indian law enforcement officers are inclined to be more lenient with intoxicated Indians than with Whites, perhaps because they think the Indians "can't help it," i.e., are constitutionally unable to handle liquor.

Since the Indian population is younger on the average than the general population (198, *p. 3*), and alcohol addiction appears to be age-related,[66] statistics should be, but seldom are, adjusted for this variable before comparisons with other populations are made. Assuming that on average it takes several years for alcohol addiction to develop (78) the comparative youth of the Indian population would have the effect of tending to understate the rate of alcohol-related crimes if arrest statistics were not adjusted, for example, by expressing a rate based on population over a certain age.

Some other problems in comparing Indian arrest rates with those of Whites are outlined by Graves (57, *pp. 37, 38*).

More general limitations on the usefulness of arrest rates as indicators of rates of aggression are applicable to any group, including Indians. The fact that a person has been arrested for a crime does not mean he was necessarily guilty of it. Conviction rates would be preferable, but are seldom used. Furthermore, all aggressive crimes are not reflected in arrests. In addition, the problem of differences in reporting practices often result in noncomparable statistics.

Despite these problems and many more, the fact remains that arrest rates are often the only available pertinent data for attempting to discover whether or not the symptom "marked aggressive behavior" occurs at a high rate among Indians in association with drinking, as is often alleged. Keeping in mind the many limitations on the validity of these arrest statistics, particularly for use in comparing Indians to other groups, as well as the fact that Indian concepts of what constitutes "aggression" may well differ from those of the dominant society, I will summarize some of the pertinent data provided in the literature on Indian alcohol use.

Some of Stewart's (184) data on national arrest rates could be incorrectly interpreted as confirming an association between alcohol and aggression among Indians. Based on F.B.I. Uniform Crime Reports for 1960, he calculated that 76% of Indian arrests were alcohol-related. However, for these national data, "alcohol-related" is defined to include only categories which by title do not seem to

[66]See, for example, Cahalan (17, *p. 42*).

directly involve aggression, i.e., "driving under the influence of alcohol," "liquor law violations," and "drunkenness."[67] Therefore, Stewart's (184, *p. 61*) often-quoted high percentage of alcohol-related crimes among Indians (76% vs 43% in the total population of the country) actually tells us nothing about the rate of alcohol-associated aggression among Indians, because the offenses identifiable in the national reports included by Stewart as alcohol-related are by title nonaggressive. The Uniform Crime Reports classify murder, forcible rape, robbery and aggravated assault as "violent" crimes (44, *p. 65, footnote 2*). These reports do not divide violent crimes into those committed under the influence of alcohol and those which are not. Violent crimes committed under the influence of alcohol thus would appear to be included in Stewart's residual category "non-alcohol-related crimes."

However, Stewart reports (184, *p. 61*) that the rate of arrest for these non-alcohol-related crimes (i.e., those other than drunkenness, driving while intoxicated, and liquor law violations) is also high among Indians, compared to the national rates. Thus, his national data do not preclude the possibility that the rate of alcohol-related violent crime is high among Indians, but this category would have to be separated from his data on non-alcohol-related crimes before we could know. (As far as I can determine, this cannot be done with the data provided by the Uniform Crime Reports used by Stewart.)

Levy and Kunitz (113, *p. 227*) note a discrepancy between Stewart's national data on non-alcohol-related crimes by Indians and their own findings in the Navaho. They report that the arrest rate for non-alcohol-related offenses and crimes tended to be low among Navahos living on and adjacent to the reservation. Since the Navaho Tribe is the largest in the U.S.A., the population observed by Levy and Kunitz represents a major portion of the one to which Stewart (184, *p. 61*) attributed a high rate of non-alcohol-related crime. Levy and Kunitz (113, *p. 227*) observe that the rate in some other Indian groups must be very high to yield a high average for Indians as a whole in spite of the low rate in the nation's largest tribe. They postulate that such variation in crime rates among Indian groups may be related to their aboriginal form of social

[67]Stewart, O. C. Personal communication, 19 August 1971.

organization.[68] Stewart suggests[67] that the apparent discrepancy might be explained in part by the fact that the Navaho are predominately rural; nationally, non-alcohol-related crimes occur at a lower rate in rural areas than in urban areas. However, Levy and Kunitz point out that Graves (57) reports low arrest rates for non-alcohol-related offenses among Navahos in an urban center (Denver).

A third explanation for the apparent discrepancy is also possible.

TABLE 3.—*Major Crimes Reported from the Navaho Indian Reservation**

| | | | Under the Influence of Alcohol | | | |
| | | | MEN | | WOMEN | |
	Men	Women	Yes	No	Yes	No
Murder	8(13?)	0	13	0	0	0
Manslaughter	4	1	4	0	1	0
Rape	15	0	14	0	0	0
Assault with intent to kill	0	0	0	0	0	0
Burglary	6	0	2	4	0	0
Arson	4	0	3	0	0	0
Larceny	4	1	1	3	1	0
Robbery	3	0	3	0	0	0
Assault with deadly weapon	41	1	36	2	0	1
Embezzlement	0	0	0	0	0	0
Incest	1	0	1	0	0	0
Extortion	1	0	0	0	0	0
Liquor violation (possession)	2	0	2	0	0	0
Assault and battery	4	0	4	0	0	0
Totals	93[a] (98?)	3[a]	83[b]	9	2[b]	1

* Major Crime Statistics, 1957, as of 9 December 1957, Navaho Indian Reservation (from Robinson, Gallup Area Office, 1958). From Stewart (184, *Table 10*).

[a] Total subjects, 96 (101?).

[b] Total under influence of alcohol, 85 = 88.5%.

[68]Levy and Kunitz (113, *p. 226*) postulate that the rates for all tribes are raised by the "hunting and gathering tribes at the family-band level of sociocultural integration," among whom, they suspect, criminality in general, but especially crimes against persons, will be high. See a similar discussion in Levy and Kunitz (112). This hypothesis is in keeping with a body of theory that insobriety is correlated with social structure, i.e., "personal (or informal) rather than a corporate (or formal) organization" (49, *p. 72*). Social structure in turn influences the effectiveness of social control, which Lemert [cit. Mandelbaum (124, *p. 291*)] considers a crucial variable in the occurrence of drinking.

If Levy and Kunitz included fewer categories of crime than Stewart under the term "non-alcohol-related," this alone might account for the variation in arrest rates for such crimes reported by each. As already pointed out, Stewart's national statistics on Indians shed no light on the degree of association between alcohol and aggression in this group. At first glance, however, his reports (184, *pp. 63-64*) by tribes or agencies (based on B.I.A. data) do seem to suggest a high association between alcohol and aggression in the groups they cover. Of all "major crimes" reported in 1957 for the Navaho Res-

TABLE 4.—*All Crimes Reported from the United Pueblo Agency**

	Men	Women	Under Influence of Alcohol		
			Yes	No	Total
Murder	4	0	4	0	4
Manslaughter	3	0	2	1	3
Rape	4	0	0	4	4
Assault with intent to kill	3	0	3	0	3
Arson	2	0	0	2	2
Burglary	16	0	13	3	16
Larceny	14	0	10	4	14
Robbery	11	0	8	3	11
Assault with dangerous weapon	11	0	10	1	11
Embezzlement	0	0	0	0	0
Incest	0	0	0	0	0
Drunkenness	113	4	117	0	117
Disorderly conduct	72	2	74	0	74
Family offenses	35	9	26	18	44
Probation violator	2	1	2	1	3
Liquor violator	53	0	52	1	53
Contempt of court	2	0	1	1	2
Assault	40	0	30	10	40
Suicide	5	0	5	0	5
Driving	18	0	18	0	18
Attempted suicide	5	1	4	2	6
Totals	413	17	379[a]	51	430

* Branch of Law and Order, United Pueblo Agency, Covering 18 Tribes of Pueblo Indians and 2 Navajo Communities (from Robinson, Gallup Area Office, 1958), Calendar Year 1957. From Stewart (184, *Table 8*).

[a] Total of criminal activity under influence of alcohol = 92%.

TABLE 5.—*"Violent" Crimes As Reported from the Navaho Reservation and the United Pueblo Agency, 1957*[*]

| | Navaho Reservation[a] | | United Pueblos Agency | |
	Total	Under Influence of Alcohol	Total	Under Influence of Alcohol
Murder	13(8?)	13	4	4
Rape	15	14	4	0
Robbery	3	3	11	8
Aggravated assault[b]				
Assault with intent to kill	0	0	3	3
Assault with deadly (dangerous) weapon	42	36	11	10
Totals	*73 (68?)*	*66*	*33*	*25*
Per cent under influence		*90 (97%)*		*76*

[*] Based on Stewart's (184, *pp. 63-64*) Tables 8 and 10, given as Tables 3 and 4 above. Numbers in parentheses are Stewart's, believed to be an error and corrected herein, together with the total.
[a] To 9 December.
[b] See definition, F.B.I. (43, *p. 22*).

ervation, 88.5% were committed under the influence of alcohol (Table 3); and of "all crimes" reported in 1957 for the United Pueblos Agency, 92% occurred while the offender was intoxicated (Table 4). However, the technical categories "major crimes" and "all crimes" include both "violent" and "nonviolent" offenses. The tables must therefore be further modified for the present purpose (Table 5).

If the comparison is limited to the crimes which fit the Uniform Crime Report category "violent," the rates are 97% in the Navaho Reservation (or 90% if I have corrected Stewart's Table 10 appropriately in the values shown in parentheses in Table 5), and 76% in the United Pueblos Agency.

Of course statistics from only two Indian groups cannot be assumed to be representative of all those covered in this study, and the difference between rates in the two groups once again illustrates the hazards of generalizing to "Indians" as a group. But, even if these rates were representative of Indians in general, are they high compared to the general U.S.A. population? Unfortunately we don't know. The Uniform Crime Reports do not provide data on the proportion of "violent" crimes committed under the influence of alcohol in the country as a whole. If we can assume that the proportion of violent crimes committed under the influence of alcohol calculated above for the Navaho is high compared to the general population, and that "aggressive" is a reasonable synonym for "violent," Stewart's data suggest a high association between alcohol and aggression in this group. However, Levy and Kunitz report a number of findings which cast doubt on the supposed association, at least in the case of homicide and suicide. Summarizing their earlier observations (115), Levy and Kunitz say (113, *p. 227*):

"Though the use of alcohol has been increasing steadily, Navajo homicide and suicide rates have remained stable as far as we can ascertain since the 1800's. Though the incidence of and deaths from alcoholic cirrhosis are significantly higher in areas near a good source of supply, i.e., off reservation and near border towns, the incidence of both homicide and suicide remains constant in all areas. While in the general White population intoxication leads to more violent forms of homicide, among the Navajo it has the opposite effect upon both homicide and suicide. When the offender is sober, suicide is more apt to be preceded by an act of homicide and sober murderers tend to shoot, stab, or beat their victims a number of times. The prior arrest records of homicide offenders are not distinguishable from those of a group of controls in respect to rates of arrest for alcohol offenses."

Graves (57, *p. 38*) objects to the conclusion he attributes to Stewart (184, *p. 64*) that arrest statistics indicate Indians are more "criminal" than other minority groups. Graves says, "they are simply more drunk." This generalization might be appropriately limited even further: perhaps Indians are simply more often arrested for drunkenness.

Stewart (184, *p. 61*) reported that 71% of Indian arrests are for simple drunkenness. Such statistics have often been interpreted as an indication of a relatively high rate of problem drinking among Indians, i.e., that Indians "are simply more drunk" than other groups. For example, a University of South Dakota report quoted by Stewart (184, *p. 66*) makes the following statement, based on arrest statistics: "a larger proportion of Indians than non-Indians drink to excess." Based on another source (144, *pp. 26–39*), Sievers (174, *p. 74*) concludes that heavy drinking "is recorded much more often for . . . Indian groups (about 36%) than for Caucasians (8.9%)." Accounts of drinking in individual Indian groups seem to confirm these generalizations. For example, Jessor (86, *p. 69*) says that without exception his measures show "a higher rate of excessive or deviance prone use of alcohol" by the Indians (Ute) than by Whites and Spanish Americans in a southwest community.

Disregarding the problem of establishing cross-culturally valid standards for "excessive," "deviance prone" and "heavy" drinking, and despite a great deal of opinion to the contrary among both Indian and White observers, I do not believe the literature on Indian drinking has so far established for most groups that Indians are "more drunk" than others, or even the degree to which Indian drinking is a problem, regardless of whether it is addictive or non-addictive. I agree rather with Keneally's appraisal (97, *p. 4*):

"What is the incidence of excessive drinking in an Indian community? How does this compare with the incidence of excessive drinking in a non-Indian community?

"In my opinion there is more confusion, misinformation and downright irrational thinking about this subject area than any other . . . concerned with Indian drinking.

"Unless we develop the protocol to accurately measure the dimension of this problem we will continue to use information based on subjective opinions rather than objective facts."

Arrest data, thus, are unlikely to provide the accurate measure of problem drinking among Indians which Keneally seeks, let alone a measure of the incidence of alcohol addiction, or even of alcohol-associated aggression.

The main difficulty encountered in attempting to investigate the relationship between alcohol and aggression is that in any community where drinking and aggressive acts occur frequently, the two are likely to co-occur, even if there is no causal relationship.

As Keller points out,[69] to qualify as a symptom of alcohol addiction, the aggressive behavior must be evoked by alcohol. Among people who experience the level of pressures and frustrations to which Indians are often subjected, this sequence might be reversed. The need to express aggression might evoke the drinking, i.e., drinking may itself be the aggressive act. If and when this is the case, whether the subject is an Indian or from some other group, the co-occurrence of drinking and aggressiveness would not qualify as a symptom of alcohol addiction in Jellinek's terms.

Evidence and opinion on the degree of association between alcohol and aggression are divided in the literature so far, not only about Indians but about the general population as well.[70] Even if the

[69]Keller, M. Personal communication, 15 March 1972.
[70]See, for example, the documentation on homicide and alcohol in Levy et al. (115, *p. 129*).

association were clear, the causal relationship would remain problematic, as already discussed. Therefore, the occurrence of Jellinek's symptom "marked aggressive behavior" under the influence of alcohol is rated CONFLICTING EVIDENCE.

13. Persistent Remorse. INSUFFICIENT EVIDENCE

Jellinek (81, *p. 681*) says that the addict's aggressive behavior inevitably "generates guilt. While even in the prodromal period remorse about the drinking arose from time to time, now *persistent remorse* . . . arises, and this added tension is a further source of drinking."

If this linkage to guilt implies that the difference in frequency suggested by the qualifying adjective "persistent" is the only criterion differentiating this symptom from Number 5, it would be rated ABSENT OR RARE; that is, if "plain" guilt does not occur, neither does "persistent" guilt. If, as seems more likely, Jellinek used "remorse" in the sense of "regret," he may have intended to emphasize feelings about the results of drinking, as opposed to those about the drinking itself. This distinction is rarely drawn in the literature; the evidence is inadequate for rating the occurrence of persistent remorse among Indians.

14. Periods of Total Abstinence: INSUFFICIENT EVIDENCE

According to Jellinek (81, *p. 681*), periods of total abstinence are used by the addict in an attempt to control his drinking "in compliance with social pressures." Since periodic (i.e., intermittent) drinking is apparently the predominant Indian pattern,[71] periods of total abstinence of course occur. However, accounts of Indian drinking do not indicate that such periods often result from efforts to control drinking, or recognition of the dangers of increasing dependence on alcohol, and certainly not from a response to social pressures which, as we have seen, are apparently decidedly weak.[72] On the contrary, periods of abstinence among Indians are often attributed to lack of money to finance drinking[73] rather than to premeditated efforts to control it. Accounts of Indian alcohol use tend to concentrate on the drinking phase of the cycle and, except for Whittaker (212, *p. 476*), say little about the abstinence phase.

Some Indians are participating in various alcoholism treatment

[71]For documentation see footnote 31.
[72]See discussion of Symptom 10 and footnotes 48, 49 and 50.
[73]Documented under Symptom 8, footnote 24.

programs.[74] They, at least, are making a conscious attempt to control their drinking. Since most of the programs include an Alcoholics Anonymous component in their composite approaches, presumably these participants are told that total abstinence is the only way an addict can control his drinking. For many participants in treatment programs, White or Indian, success in the pursuit of abstinence is only partial—they experience periodic "slips," and thus their abstinence pattern is periodic, too.

Like many of the tenets of Alcoholics Anonymous, abstinence may be foreign to the values of Indians. As the results of tribal treatment programs become more available, we will be able to judge how widespread such learned attitudes may have become. The following item illustrates attitudes toward Alcoholics Anonymous in general, and toward its tenet of abstinence in particular, which I have sometimes encountered in field work among Nevada Indians. The report quotes the comments of a Deputy Director of the Nevada Inter-Tribal Council on the methods of a White director of the ITC alcoholism program who had been dismissed the previous month:

"I felt that his methods were too close to those of Alcoholics Anonymous. . . . Rather than require complete abstinence from alcohol, we'd rather teach social or controlled drinking. I have no criticism of A.A. but I don't think their methods work with Indians."[75]

This suggests that consciously "going on the wagon" is not likely to become a common device for controlling excessive drinking, among Nevada Indians at least, but for the other groups covered herein we have very little direct evidence on the occurrence of such behavior. On the other hand, the popularity of disulfiram (Antabuse) treatment in some Indian programs (e.g., 47, p. 160; 88, p. 9) suggests that the notion of abstinence may have begun to diffuse into some groups, but with adaptations—a common occurence when a foreign element is incorporated into a culture.

That pressure to drink is extremely strong in some Indian groups has already been noted.[76] Refusal of an invitation to join a drinking party, or even to accept a drink, is said to be a deep personal insult. Taking disulfiram has provided a means of counteracting this pressure in some groups. Drinking companions are aware (perhaps

---

[74]For some accounts of these programs, see Ferguson (46, 47, 48); Henderson (65); Jicarilla Apache Alcoholism Project (88); Martinez (127); Savard (169); Spang (180); Szuter et al. (187); Toler (191); Werner (209).

[75]*Nevada State Journal*, 10 August 1971.

[76]Documented in footnote 48.

exaggeratedly) of the unplesant consequences of combining "Ant-abuse" and alcohol. Thus, if they know a person is "on the pill" they no longer regard refusal as an affront and leave the ex-drinker in peace. Given these circumstances, in Indian groups the use of disul-firam might be efficacious for the nonaddict who simply wishes to change his drinking habits, although in the dominant society it is usually indicated for the "addict" only. In addition to this practical modification of the normal use of disulfiram, Indians might find it has a "magical" function, as it seems to have for some addicts in the dominant society.[77]

15. Changing the Pattern of Drinking: INSUFFICIENT EVIDENCE

Another method of control employed by dominant-society addicts is to change the pattern of their drinking, "by setting up rules about not drinking before a certain hour of the day, in certain places only, and so forth" (81, *p. 681*). This behavior seems closely connected to the 9-to-5, 5-day week steady-employment orientation of the domi-nant society. When people have no jobs for drinking to interfere with, as many Indians do not, one incentive for limiting the time and place of drinking could be absent. Furthermore, employment seems to be far less important to the self-image and community status of many Indians than it is to Whites (e.g., *74, p. 222; 161, pp. 4, 5*). Thus, the exigencies of a job as an incentive to control drinking may be weaker among Indians than among Whites.

If Indians are less preoccupied with time than Whites (e.g., *161, pp. 2, 3, 4; 116, pp. 71, 72*), the likelihood of the occurrence of this symptom among them may be further decreased. And since social sanctions against drinking are weak (see Symptom 10), one might infer that avoidance of criticism as an intermediate motive for chang-ing the pattern of drinking would also be lacking. Whittaker (212, *p. 476*) reports that 76% of a random sample of the Standing Rock Sioux had tried to control their drinking by changing the ways they drink. This is the only evidence I have encountered which seems directly pertinent to the symptom.

16. Drop Friends: INSUFFICIENT EVIDENCE

The strain of the addict's struggle to control his drinking "increases his hostility towards his environment and he begins to *drop friends*.

[77]Keller, M. Personal communication, 15 March 1972.

... It goes without saying that some associates drop him ... but more frequently he takes the initiative as an anticipatory defence" (81, *p. 681*). For most Indian groups covered herein there appears to be general agreement that little or no rejection occurs for the drinker to anticipate.[78] Therefore it might be inferred that there would be little incentive to drop friends in this group. However, since there is no direct evidence on this behavior in the literature, it is rated INSUFFICIENT EVIDENCE.

16A. *Solitary Drinking:* CONFLICTING EVIDENCE

I have added solitary drinking to Jellinek's list. Though he does not specifically include it as a symptom of alcohol addiction, it seems clear that he considered it to be an important feature of addicts' behavior from the "system of isolation" which he discusses (81, *p. 680*), from other symptoms on the list such as "drop friends" (Symptom 16), and from his inclusion of solitary drinking as a symptom of alcohol addiction in an earlier version of his phases study (*78, pp. 48, 49, 50*).

Keller[77] points out that only solitary *"drunking"* (rather than "drinking") should be considered a symptom of alcohol addiction. Solitary *"drunking"* could even take place in the presence of others who might be drinking (e.g., in a bar, but not associating with the subject), or who might not be drinking.

Solitary drinking has been added to the list of symptoms because a few proponents of the reverse-firewater hypothesis seem to rely heavily on its absence to justify their view that alcohol addiction is absent or rare among Indians. For example, Berreman (10, *p. 511*) seems to offer the absence of solitary drinking as one of the main justifications for his statement that "there have been no observed or reported cases of true alcoholism, of compulsive or addictive drinking" in the Aleut group he reports upon. Dozier's (36, *p. 72*) juxtaposition of the absence of lone drinkers with the rarity of addicted drinkers suggests that he considers the absence of solitary drinking to be an important justification for his conclusion that addiction is "perhaps less common among Indians than among other groups." Lemert's (107, *p. 362*) statement that "Seldom will an Indian drink alone if he can avoid it, even a heavy drinker," seems to be an integral part of his conclusion that "although excessive sustained

[78]See the discussion at Symptom 10 and footnote 50.

drunkenness occurs in Coastal Indians, it is symptomatic rather than compulsive or addictive in nature." A Bureau of Indian Affairs community planner—cited by Officer (152, *p. 5*)—also juxtaposes a statement that "it is inconceivable for them to think about drinking alone" and the opinion that "with the exception of one person there are probably no alcoholics in the tribe," which Officer (152, *p. 4*) describes as an "isolated Indian community . . . notorious for its high consumption of alcoholic beverages."

North American Indian drinking is almost universally described as social.[79] In context, this characteristic is frequently contrasted with solitary drinking, which is often said to be absent or rare among them.[80] Several observers, however, present convincing evidence that solitary drinking does occur in Indian groups.[81] Perhaps this behavior has not been reported more frequently simply because it

[79]Berreman (10, *p. 506*); Clairmont (23, *p. 57*); Clark (24, *p. 6*); Curley (27, *p. 120*); Devereux (33, *p. 210*); Dozier (36, *p. 72*); Ferguson (48, *p. 900*); Graves (57, *p. 39*); Hamer (58, *p. 289*); Heath (62, *pp. 16, 63*); Honigmann and Honigmann (68, *p. 590*); Keneally (97, *p. 3*); Kuttner and Lorincz (103, *p. 533*); Lemert (107, *pp. 310, 362, 363; 108, p. 92*); Littman (116, *p. 70*); Sanchez (168, *p. 2*); Savard (169, *p. 911*); Washburne (208, *p. 179*).

[80]Berreman (10, *p. 506*); B.I.A. community planner cited by Officer (152 *p. 4*); Curley (27, *p. 120*); Dailey (28, *pp. 22, 25*); Dozier (36, *p. 72*); Ferguson (47, p. *163*); Hamer (58, *p. 289*); Heath (63, *pp. 123, 129*); Honigmann and Honigmann (68, *p. 590; 69, p. 225*); Keneally (97, *p. 3*); Kuttner and Lorincz (103, *p. 536*); Lemert (107, *pp. 310, 362–363; 108, p. 92*); Littman (116, *p. 71; 117, p. 1778*); Maynard (129, *p. 43*); Savard (169, *p. 911*).

[81]For example, Boyce (13, *p. 25*) reports that 28 of 152 Indian high-school boys in his sample admitted drinking alone at times. Clairmont (22, *p. 2; 23, p. 57*) says that lone drinking does occur "in the bush," though most drinking is done in groups. Du Toit (38, *p. 18*) refers to a category of "lonely drinkers" who are not recognized by the 2 other groups ("party drinkers" and "nondrinkers"). Hurt and Brown (74, *p. 229*) contrast the South American Camba, whose drinking is exclusively social, to the Dakota who, they say, "may drink as solitary individuals." Slater's (239, *p. 20*) group of Uintah-Ouray who had been arrested for drinking reported solitary drinking as follows: sometimes, 27%; often, 6%; yes, most of the time, 14%. Of Whittaker's (212, *p. 476*) random sample of Standing Rock Sioux, 10% reported drinking alone. Levy and Kunitz (113, *p. 232*) say the high death rate from cirrhosis among the Hopi, noted for their sobriety and lack of public drinking, "indicates the presence of a considerable amount of steady covert drinking." Kunitz et al. (102, *p. 717*) report that "many Hopi drinkers report solitary drinking as a means of avoiding social censure." Levy and Kunitz (112, *p. 117*) say that "the Hopi tend to hide their drinking from the village, to drink in solitude and in bars."

is relatively more difficult to observe than public social drinking.

Levy and Kunitz (113, *p. 223*) say it took them several years of field work before they observed private family drinking; presumably clandestine solitary drinking would be even more unlikely to be observed. In fact, these authors (113, *p. 223*) explicitly note that since covert forms of drinking are difficult to observe directly, "the anthropologist must make inferences concerning them based upon general statements made about these acts by his informants. As such statements may be normative explanations themselves, they frequently do not describe the reality with any degree of accuracy."

Despite the difficulties of observation, these authors (e.g., 102, *p. 717*) have reported data suggesting that solitary drinking actually does occur more frequently among the Hopi than among their Navaho neighbors. The occurrence of solitary drinking among the Hopi may reflect the presence in this group of stronger social sanctions than have been reported as the norm in many other groups (see Symptom 10), as well as a distinct method of social control (ejection of problem drinkers from the community).

Cahalan et al. (18, *p. 89*) doubt that solitary drinking is a valid indicator of problem drinking in the general population. "It may well be that many of those who drink alone [principally older, less well-to-do persons] do so only because there is no one at hand with whom to drink." However, considering the cultural forces which would seem to discourage most Indians from solitary drinking (with the Hopi exception noted above), its occurrence would perhaps seem more implicative of "trouble" among Indians than among Whites. This possibility, coupled with the difficulties of detecting such behavior, might tempt one to attach special importance to the few positive reports available on Indians (as discussed in Chapter 5).

For the moment, the reports will simply be tallied. I have assigned the statements in the literature on the occurrence of solitary drinking to the two rating categories PRESENT (7 "accounts") and ABSENT–RARE (15 "accounts")[82] and have assigned an over-all rating of CONFLICTING EVIDENCE to this "symptom." Ideally, a definite rating of ABSENT–RARE should be confined to cases in which the incidence of a symptom is clearly less than in the general population; the rating PRESENT should be supported by evidence that the incidence is at least as great as in the dominant society. However, few

[82]Calculated from footnotes 80 and 81 in accordance with the method described in footnote 15, chapter 4, as shown in Chart 2, *p. 110.*

authors attempt to estimate rates in the Indian groups they report upon, and there are no firm estimates for the general population, either. Therefore, the rating of the occurrence of this symptom in individual groups has involved a great deal of interpretation, with which the authors cited might disagree. For example, Du Toit (38, *p. 19*) says a "few" individuals drink alone among the Klamath group. The town he reports upon had a population of 110 Indians. Taking 3 as a minimum definition of "a few," this yields a proportion of solitary drinkers in the group which does not seem negligible when compared with estimates of 4% for the number of alcohol addicts in the general population (199, *p. 10*). On this basis, I rated the symptom PRESENT among the Klamath. However, the proper comparison would be with the proportion of the general population who are *solitary drinkers* rather than addicts—statistics that do not exist. Slightly different interpretation of some of the pertinent statements might have tipped the balance enough to yield a summary rating of PRESENT or ABSENT–RARE, instead of CONFLICTING EVIDENCE—the rating I have assigned. Culture-area distribution of the supporting citations is shown in Chart 2 on page 110.

17. *Quit Jobs:* INSUFFICIENT EVIDENCE

Jellinek (81, *p. 681*) says that this behavior, like "dropping friends" (Symptom 16), occurs as an anticipatory defense. Certainly Indians are frequently dismissed from jobs or not hired as a result of drinking.[83] Therefore, in contrast to rejection by friends, being fired seems to present a real possibility to be anticipated. It also appears that some Indians take a cavalier attitude toward their jobs (e.g., 103, *p. 540*), quitting or being absent when work interferes with other activities they value (such as ceremonies, hunting and, possibly, drinking) more frequently than the norm in dominant-society workers. But so far there seems to be no indication that anticipation of being fired for drinking figures among the motives for voluntarily interrupting employment. However, mere lack of such evidence is not a reliable indication that this behavior does not occur.

18. *Behavior becomes Alcohol-Centered:* INSUFFICIENT EVIDENCE

Jellinek (81, *p. 681*) describes this behavior as follows: "The isolation becomes more pronounced as his entire *behavior becomes al-*

[83]American Indian workshop (222, *p. 3*); Clairmont (23, *p. 66*); Graves (57, *p. 44*); Medicine (130, *p. 19*); Robbins (162, *p. 71*); Slater (238, *p. 20*).

cohol-centered . . . i.e. he begins to be concerned about how activities might interfere with his drinking instead of how his drinking may affect his activities. This, of course, involves a more marked egocentric outlook which leads to more rationalizations and more isolation." Since Jellinek seems to consider "alcohol-centered behavior" to be contingent on social "isolation," which has been rarely reported to be experienced by Indian problem drinkers, one might infer that this symptom would also be rare among Indians. However, in accordance with previous discussions, I reject the alternative of assigning definite ratings of occurrence on the basis of this inference.

A few statements in the literature tend to indicate that Indians rarely behave in the fashion described by Jellinek. For example, Dailey (28, *p. 26*) says that Indians "are not gripped with that iron-willed compulsion to seek alcohol in ways characteristic of alcoholics in our society." Berreman (10, *p. 511*) saw no evidence of pathological desire for alcohol among the Aleut group he studied, and Lemert (107, *p. 362*) makes similar observations concerning Northwest Coast Indians. These remarks might be interpreted as suggesting that alcohol-centered behavior is absent or rare among the Indian groups in question. However, these statements might also be interpreted as referring to absence of "preoccupation with alcohol" (Symptom 3), or of alcohol addiction in general. But, regardless of how they are interpreted, there are too few statements pertinent to the occurrence of alcohol-centered behavior to justify assigning it a rating.

19. Loss of Outside Interests: INSUFFICIENT EVIDENCE

The literature on Indian drinking often suggests that drinking parties are the main source of recreation and social interaction, particularly on reservations. Some reports suggest that lack of recreational opportunities encourages problem drinking.[84] Indians are sometimes reported to agree.[85] If by "outside interests" Jellinek had in mind recreation, these statements suggest that Indians may have few "outside interests" to lose.

Whittaker (213, *p. 84*) asked a random sample of Standing Rock Sioux, "What is there to do with your free time?" The replies were as follows: nothing, 31%; hobbies, 18%; activities with children, 18%;

[84]Documented in footnote 47.
[85]See footnote 40.

chores, 27%; drink, 3%; miscellaneous, 3%. These replies tend to support the notion that recreational opportunities for Indians are meager, but the small proportion who indicate that drinking provides a substitute does not seem to reinforce the "recreational" theory of Indian alcoholism in the group studied.

The notion of a dichotomy between "work" and "outside," and the implication that the latter is a secondary activity, appears to be an unlikely candidate for a cultural universal. Yet the assumption that all people divide their activities into these two spheres seems to underlie the interpretation of "loss of outside interests" as a symptom of alcohol addiction.

20. Reinterpretation of Interpersonal Relationships: CONFLICTING EVIDENCE

One might be tempted to infer that there would be no need for Indian problem drinkers to reinterpret interpersonal relationships (81, *p. 681*), since they apparently are not rejected by their families and communities and are excused for their drunken transgressions in most groups.[86] Moreover, some observers explicitly deny that heavy drinking leads, for example, to broken marriages or loss of family in the groups they report upon.[87]

On the other hand, some works indicate that public officials, at least, may jeopardize their positions in Indian communities by drinking, and some studies suggest that insobriety does indeed lead to strained relationships with families and other Indians.[88] For example, in a sample of Uintah-Ouray who had been jailed for drinking, 8% reported they had lost their mates and children because of drinking and 41% reported that drinking had "caused them to have problems with other people" (239, *p. 16*).

It seems likely that when drinking temporarily interferes with a person's ability to fulfill the role expectations which others hold for him, some adjustment must occur, even if the drinker is not rejected. This subject, it seems to me, would be of ethnographic interest even for observers whose primary focus is not the study of drinking. The present literature on Indian drinking, however, seems very thin on this point.

[86]See footnotes 49 and 50.
[87]E.g., Lemert (107, *p. 314;* 108, *pp. 102, 104*); Whittaker (213, *p. 85*).
[88]E.g., Collins (25, *p. 112*); Curley (27, *p. 124*); Lemert (108, *p. 105*).

21. Marked Self-Pity: INSUFFICIENT EVIDENCE

As already noted, the evidence on behavioral changes resulting from drinking is equivocal in the literature on Indian alcohol use. Direct references to self-pity seem to be absent. The only statements which seem even vaguely pertinent present a conflicting picture. Medicine (130, *p. 10*) says that during Dakota drinking bouts a maudlin sentimentality prevails and is often a prelude to the onset of hostility and bellicosity. On the other hand, Heath (63, *p. 126*) noted only one instance of such behavior among the Navaho, and Devereux (33, *p. 215*) explicitly remarked on its complete absence among the Mohave. In any case, I don't suppose "maudlin sentimentality" is necessarily an equivalent of "marked self-pity."

Jellinek (81, *p. 681*) provided no standard for the qualifying adjective "marked." The fact that many Indians have legitimate reasons to feel sorry for themselves would no doubt complicate an investigation of the incidence of this behavior among them, and the validity of interpreting it as a symptom of alcohol addiction among Indians is certainly open to question, even if more evidence were available.

If Indian problem drinkers are not rejected, there seems to be no reason for them to feel self-pity in connection with their drinking, but I have rejected the alternative of basing a rating of this symptom on such an inference, in accordance with previous discussions.

22. Geographic Escape: INSUFFICIENT EVIDENCE

By the time the symptoms so far discussed have appeared, Jellinek (81, *p. 681*) says, "The isolation and rationalizations have increased . . . in intensity and find their expression either in contemplated or actual *geographic escape.*" In the earliest version of his phases study Jellinek (78, *p. 63*) said that geographic escape was reported by only 63% of the 98 male A.A. members on which that report was based. He remarked that such behavior does not appear to be as essential a characteristic of alcohol addiction as many other symptoms, and probably is "a rather minor manifestation of some essential element," such as rationalization.

The literature contains very little evidence or even opinion on the occurrence of geographic escape in association with drinking among Indians. Lemert (108, *p. 104*) suggests that changes in residence are oriented toward a supply of alcohol rather than away from censure. Slotkin (175, *p. 15*) says the nondrinkers are more likely than the drinkers to leave the reservation. Chance (20, *p. 1032*) explicitly notes that he found only one case of ejection for drinking from the Eskimo community he studied, but this group in any case was cited as having made an exceptional adjustment to modern life.

On the other hand, Kunitz et al. (e.g., 101, *p. 683*) say that disruptive drinking may "lead to the ejection of the deviant individual from the more integrated rural community" of the Hopi. They base this opinion on evidence that all deaths from cirrhosis among Hopis occurred in the border towns among persons who had had long histories of drinking prior to leaving their reservation communities. Ejection from a community, however, is not the same as a deliberate decision to go away in order to control drinking problems. In any group, it would seem to be difficult to distinguish mobility which qualifies as a symptom of alcohol addiction from mobility which is merely dictated by circumstances or personality problems not necessarily related to drinking.

Geographic escape as a means of avoiding problems created by heavy drinking would seem to merit more observation among Indians. Such investigations would be complicated by the task of sorting out this motive from others for leaving the reservation; comparisons of incidence would have to take into account different rates of mobility among Indians as compared with the dominant society.

In most groups, absence of social sanctions against drinking and the tendency not to reject problem drinkers would seem to minimize the incentive for leaving the community because of problem drinking. However, I have not relied on such an inference in rating this symptom and have chosen to include geographic escape in the category for which the evidence seems insufficient to judge its occurrence among Indians.

23. *Change in Family Habits:* INSUFFICIENT EVIDENCE

This symptom is exhibited by the family of the addict, not by the addict himself. Jellinek (81, *p. 681*) says: "The wife and children, who may have had good social activities, may withdraw for fear of embarrassment or, quite contrarily, they may suddenly begin intensive outside activities in order to escape from the home environment."

All the other symptoms described by Jellinek are exhibited by the afflicted person. It may seem strange to include the reaction of associates as a separate diagnostic sign of alcohol addiction. However, by doing so, Jellinek anticipated one of the main points of a recent contribution to our understanding of the process of alcohol addiction. Bacon (4) emphasizes the role of "others" in teaching and enforcing social controls over drinking. He notes (4, *p. 15*) that previously "the dominant thrust in both theory and action, whether in relation to etiology, treatment or prevention, has been the individual." This focus, by itself, is inadequate for an understanding of the problem, he says. "The roles and activities of 'others' appear to manifest highly cogent, if not indeed essential, elements . . . Loss of control, from this viewpoint, is a phenomenon involving both the actor and others, a phenomenon involving learning (and un-learning) through time" (*p. 16*).

With this background he presents a view (4, *pp. 18–24*) of both the development of alcoholism and the process of recovery therefrom as a "progressive disjunction between the labelings of others and the alcoholic candidate." In the direction of alcoholism, the alcoholic's labeling of his stage of development lags behind that of others. In the direction of recovery, others are slower than the alcoholic to revise their labeling of the extent of progress. Bacon (4, *pp. 23, 24*) then explores the implications of this perspective for revising our ideas about the setting, personnel, methods and evaluation of treatment, as well as for prevention. Regarding the latter, he says, the approach

"suggests that a major arena to be attacked is the disjunctive labeling process on the way into alcoholism. It suggests that the 'others,' those surrounding important persons in Bill's life when he first started to deviate in any repetitive patterned fashion could have responded differently, could have behaved in ways which would diminish the chances of Bill's actions and attitudes, and their own actions and attitudes, resulting in that downward spiral of dissocialization, desocialization and loss of self- and social controls with the accompanying enhancement of the nonsocial functions of alcohol ingestion. Rather than attacking Bill, or attacking Booze, or attacking weak or sick personalities or livers or enzymatic functions or even the vast system called the drinking custom as such, this hypothesized aspect of the alcoholism process, without denying the values or possible utility of any of those approaches, suggests a very different quality and very different target for the preventive process" (*p. 26*).

This short summary necessarily oversimplifies Bacon's contribution and the many qualifications he attaches to the main points outlined here. However, I hope I have adequately suggested the pertinence of Bacon's contribution not only to the symptom in question but also to the whole concept of alcohol addiction.

In the literature on Indian drinking, there is unfortunately very little direct evidence on the potentially interesting subject of "change in family habits" associated with drinking. Emphasis on working with families, in addition to the drinker, in treatment programs (e.g., 88, pp. 11, 12; 179, p. 21) suggests that families do react to the drinker's behavior, but these accounts provide no details about the manner or degree of the manifestations. Furthermore, a number of authors report that family members, especially the wife, are the predominant objects of drunken aggression in several groups,[89] even where the frequency of aggression is inversely proportional to the frequency of drinking together (62, p. 77). If so, this would seem to provide a dramatic incentive for changes in the habits of the families of problem drinkers. On the other hand, as already noted above (Symptom 20), a few authors deny that the Indian problem drinker's behavior jeopardizes his marriage or family life.

Family reaction to the behavior of the drinker would seem to merit more observation than the literature now reflects, if only as a matter of general ethnographic interest, whether or not the reactions are interpreted as evidence of alcohol addiction in the family member who generates them.

24. Unreasonable Resentments: INSUFFICIENT EVIDENCE

Jellinek (81, p. 681) says that the family's pattern of adjustment, as well as "other events," lead to the onset of unreasonable resentments in the alcohol addict, but no standard for measuring "unreasonable" is provided. In his earlier version of the phases study, Jellinek (78, p. 4) cited an example provided by the A.A. members who devised the original questionnaire: "Going into a rage because dinner wasn't ready the minute you got home."

Thus far the literature sheds no light on the occurrence of this symptom among Indians.

Attempts to investigate the more general question of the Indian drinker's reaction to his own behavior have produced disappoint-

---

[89]Hamer (58, p. 285); Honigmann and Honigmann (68, p. 600; 70, p. 75); Kaplan (235) cited by Whittaker (213, p. 83); Kuttner and Lorincz (103, p. 539); Lemert (108, pp. 93, 95, 100); Levy (110, p. 311); Levy et al. (115, p. 137) [homicides, not necessarily under the influence of alcohol]; Robbins (162, p. 157); Slotkin (175, p. 14).

ing results. For example, Whittaker (213, *p. 86*) asked his Standing Rock Sioux sample, "How do you feel after a drinking party or spree?" The responses were as follows: no answer, 65%; "rugged, lousy, sick," 19%; "guilty," 15%; "nothing at all," 1%. Slater's (238, *p. 15*) Uintah-Ouray sample of arrested drinkers responded as follows to the question "Do you feel that excessive drinking is a problem for you": no, 29%; I don't know, 25%; occasionally, 22%; I think so, 14%; yes, 10%. Both Whittaker and Slater used questionnaires to gather their data. In the literature on Indian drinking the studies based on questionnaires, as a general rule, cover more topics than those based on participant observation, but, as the responses quoted above illustrate, the depth of coverage leaves something to be desired.

The only bit of evidence I have encountered suggestive of unreasonable resentment is an account of one Indian A.A. member who accused another of spying on her to see whether she had "slipped" (224, *p. 1*). The A.A. affiliation may be a significant factor in this instance. However, negative evidence does not justify the conclusion that such behavior does not occur, and I do not consider it appropriate to infer the absence of this symptom from the absence of guilt and social sanctions, as already discussed.

25. *Protect Liquor Supply:* INSUFFICIENT EVIDENCE

Jellinek (81, *p. 681*) describes this symptom as follows: "The predominance of concern with alcohol induces the addict to *protect his supply* . . . i.e., to lay in a large stock of alcoholic beverages, hidden in the most unthought-of places. A fear of being deprived of the most necessary substance for his living is expressed in this behavior."

A few studies provide evidence which seems related to the premeditation described by Jellinek. For example, at Frobisher Bay, the Eskimo instituted a 3-week waiting period between order and pick-up at the liquor store. Consumption, public drunkenness and arrests dropped markedly. An informant could not explain why drinkers did not order beverages 3 weeks in advance of delivery. "He simply treated the idea as preposterous when he said people want to drink when they want to drink" (70, *p. 77*). The observers point out that the same people exhibit the ability to plan in other activities but, for them, drinking apparently is highly spontaneous. This might suggest that hoarding liquor in the manner described by Jellinek is unlikely to occur, at least in this group. Some Eskimo did buy alcohol for delivery 3 weeks later, but there is no indication that problem drinking or the motive of protecting liquor supply was a common characteristic of the group.

Home brew requires time to "work," yet the accounts of groups which rely on such local production for their alcohol supply do not indicate any attempt to maintain a constant supply. Rather, when a brew is ready, or even before, according to Honigmann and Honigmann (68, *p. 588*) and Lemert (107, *p. 309*), it is consumed in one bout, shared with friends (e.g., 10, *pp. 506, 507; 7, p. 191*). There is no indication that preparation of the next batch begins, or is even planned, soon after the supply is gone. The brew is carefully protected from detection by the police and from theft by other Indians (61, *p. 10; 107, p. 309*), but the motive seems to be to conserve it for chosen friends rather than to assure a supply for the brewer.

These accounts make it clear that the etiquette of sharing, already described, is sometimes circumvented, or at least applies only to certain relationships. Within these relationships, it does appear that social ostracism is a far higher risk for the hoarder of alcohol than for the drunkard (e.g., 22, *p. 2; 33, p. 210*). But in other relationships the sharing etiquette appears to be so flexible it would not preclude the occurrence of the symptom "protect liquor supply." Therefore, it seems unjustified to rate this symptom ABSENT–RARE on the basis of inference from the etiquette of sharing. The direct evidence suggesting the presence of the symptom is too meager to justify a rating of occurrence, and mere lack of evidence is not a reliable indication that the symptom does not occur.

26. *Neglect of Proper Nutrition:* INSUFFICIENT EVIDENCE

Ideas of "proper" nutrition are obviously in part culture-specific but, presumably, some minimum standards would have cross-cultural validity. Assuming that such standards were available, investigation of the incidence among Indians of inadequate nutrition associated with alcohol use is complicated by several factors. The poverty prevalent in many Indian groups makes it difficult to know whether an individual is undernourished because drinking leads him to neglect food or because he cannot afford an adequate diet. It is difficult to observe food intake with sufficient accuracy to serve as an indirect basis for judgment on this point, and I imagine it is hard to decide with certainty that a particular physical manifestation is attributable to inadequate nourishment. Furthermore, as Lemert

(107, *p. 341*) comments regarding the Homalthko, "examinations reveal past and present malnutrition. . . . Whether this was a direct or indirect effect of their excessive drinking, of course, the physician could not say." Perhaps such problems of data collection and interpretation account for the dearth of evidence on the incidence of malnutrition associated with alcohol use among Indians.

27. *Hospitalization, Alcoholic Cirrhosis:* PRESENT

Jellinek (81, *p. 681*) says that neglect of proper nutrition aggravates the beginning of the effects of heavy drinking on the organism, and frequently the addict is first hospitalized for "some alcoholic complaint" at this time. Unfortunately, Jellinek does not indicate what disorders he intends the term to cover. Neither "hospitalization" nor "alcoholic complaint" seem to qualify as unitary symptoms or to be likely categories for medical reporting. Nevertheless, physicians probably can identify alcohol-related complaints from hospital records without too much difficulty. Thus, theoretically, it should be easier to gather data on this symptom than on most of the others. However, little information on the incidence of such maladies has found its way into the literature on Indian drinking. Laënnec's cirrhosis is mentioned more frequently than other alcohol-related disorders, not only in the literature on Indian drinking but in the general alcohol literature as well. The rating for hospitalization herein is based on the reported occurrence of cirrhosis in these statements.

Reviewing the evidence that Laënnec's cirrhosis reflects excessive alcohol consumption, Kunitz et al. (101, *p. 673*) say: "It is clear that cirrhosis of the liver (so called Laënnec's or alcoholic cirrhosis) is related to excessive alcohol consumption. This has been determined experimentally and epidemiologically, and is also a common clinical observation. Nevertheless, the precise nature of the relationship is still not understood." In addition to high alcohol intake, other mechanisms may play a role in the etiology, including inherited resistance (or susceptibility) and an interaction between alcohol and viral hepatitis. However, inherited factors do not seem to account for the cirrhosis rates found by Kunitz et al. (101, *p. 683*) among the Navaho, nor does hepatitis, since the Navaho have a high incidence of the latter disease but a slightly low incidence of alcoholic cirrhosis (*p. 674*). They further observe: "In general, it is not difficult to distinguish between posthepatitis and Laënnec's cirrhosis both on clinical and pathological grounds, and we are herein assuming the accuracy of the diagnosis." They conclude that, "For the purposes of the present report it is assumed that cases of Laënnec's cirrhosis are a reflection of excessive alcohol consumption." The other authorities whose statistics on the incidence of cirrhosis in various Indian groups are cited herein appear to make the same assumption, but the type of cirrhosis being reported is not always clear.

The most extensive data on the incidence of alcoholic cirrhosis among Indians are supplied by Levy and Kunitz in a number of papers concerning the Navaho, Hopi and Apache.

Kunitz et al. (102, *p. 715*) report that the cirrhosis mortality per 100,000 population (age adjusted, 1965–66) is slightly lower among the Navaho (13.0 to 17.0, depending on the population estimate used) than in the general population (19.9). On the other hand, the rates among the White Mountain Apache (44.0) and the Hopi (104.0) greatly exceeded the national rates. Among the Hopi, Levy and Kunitz (112) report an apparent connection between cirrhosis rates and the degree of social pressure against drinking. They detect a gradient of social sanctions against drinking in this group: high in villages where traditional theocratic social controls remain strong, and low in villages where dominant-society methods prevail and controls are relatively weak. This gradient seems to be negatively correlated with the incidence of cirrhosis: absent in the traditional villages, from which deviant drinkers are ejected; and high both in off-reservation towns, to which some ejected drinkers eventually migrate, and in the more modern villages which are the initial target for most ejected migrants and where problem drinkers evidently are allowed to remain. These within-tribe comparisons underscore the dangers of generalizing about the occurrence or incidence of a symptom of alcohol addiction in a single Indian group, much less in North American Indians as a whole.

A few other authors report the occurrence of "cirrhosis" in a number of Indian groups,[90] but most of them provide insufficient detail for comparison either with the Levy and Kunitz findings or with data on the general population. Only 8 "accounts" of the occurrence of cirrhosis were found in the literature, and a majority of these con-

[90]IHS Task Force (75, *p. 10*); Kunitz et al. (101, *p. 678*; 102, *p. 714*); Levy and Kunitz (111, *pp. 16–18*; 113, *p. 231*); Littman (117, *pp. 1770–1771*) citing Harris and Harris (60); Reichenbach (160, *p. 84*); Savard (169, *p. 914*); Sievers (174, *p. 77*); Slater (238, *p. 18*) [" liver problems"]; U.S.H.E.W. (198, *p. 16*).

cern the Navaho.[91] Only 2 of Driver and Massey's (37) 9 pertinent culture areas are covered by the statements which generalize about individual groups (Table 2). However, the main basis for rating the symptom PRESENT is the Public Health Service report (198, *p. 16*) covering American Indians as a whole, based on statistics compiled by the National Vital Statistics Division, reporting death rates in 1964 from cirrhosis as 26.7 per 100,000 among Indians and 12.8 per 100,000 in all races (not age-adjusted). Thus all community types are represented (Table 2 and Appendix).

The relationship between cirrhosis and alcoholism was used by Jellinek (219, *Annex 2*) as the basis for a formula by which he estimated the number of alcoholics in the nation from the reported deaths from cirrhosis of the liver. Keller (90, *p. 5*) describes the theory underlying the formula[92] as follows:

"In the absence of direct means of determining objectively the number of alcoholics, E. M. Jellinek devised a formula whereby the number of 'alcoholics with complications'—those who exhibit a diagnosable physical or psychological change due to prolonged excessive drinking—can be estimated from the reported deaths from cirrhosis of the liver. The principle of the formula rests on Jellinek's determination of the constant relationship between the percentage of alcoholics . . . who die of cirrhosis of the liver and the proportion of all deaths from cirrhosis attributable to alcoholism. Once the number of alcoholics with complications is thus calculated, another constant is required to allow the addition of alcoholics without complications. This latter constant varies from country to country. In the United States and Canada, according to Jellinek, it is 4; that is, there are 3 alcoholics without for every alcoholic with complications, hence the number with complications must be multiplied by 4 to obtain the total number of alcoholics."

Both the theoretical basis and the constants of the formula have

[91]Footnote 90 contains 11 citations documenting that Hospitalization, Alcoholic cirrhosis (Symptom 27) is PRESENT in the groups covered. Of these, 8 qualify as "accounts": (60), (75), (101, 102, 111 and 113), (117), (160), (169), (174), (198).

[92]The formula is expressed as follows [based on Keller (90, *p. 5*)]: $R(PD/K) = A$ when $R =$ the ratio of all alcoholics to alcoholics with complications, $P =$ the percentage of deaths from cirrhosis of the liver in a given year attributable to alcoholism, $D =$ the number of reported deaths from cirrhosis of the liver in a given year, $K =$ the percentage of all "alcoholics with complications" who die of cirrhosis of the liver, and $A =$ the total number of alcoholics alive in a given year (in a given group). The values of the constants first established by Jellinek (219, *Annex 2*) were revised by him in 1949 (80) and 1959 (83). It should be noted that Jellinek established different values of P for men and women.

been criticized.[93] A recent Public Health Service publication dismisses the formula summarily (199, *p. 10*); but Keller (91, *p. 320*) believes that "the underlying theory . . .—that alcoholism is reflected in mortality from liver cirrhosis—is beyond dispute," and Popham (158, *p. 591*) found that "the various empirical confirmations justify substantial confidence in the Jellinek estimation formula."

Although Levy and Kunitz might have used the Jellinek formula to estimate the number of alcoholics in the Indian groups they studied, they specifically declined (101, *p. 677*), confining their analysis to a comparison of cirrhosis mortality rates among the tribes and with the national rates. This decision was prudent for a number of reasons. Even though there may be nothing inherently wrong with the idea underlying the formula, the mathematical relationships represented by the constants need to be updated for the dominant society before they are applied to more recent data; it is not possible to be sure the constants would be the same for Indians, and, most important, the formula was never applicable to small populations.[94] Keller points out further that it would be desirable for investigators to report their data separately by sex, since the incidence and mortality rates vary between men and women, as recognized by Jellinek (219, *Annex 2*) when he provided a different value of P for each sex in his formula. However, Kunitz et al. (102, *p. 714*) found no significant differences in fatality rate between the sexes among the Navaho and Hopi.

As the foregoing discussion probably illustrates, the collection and evaluation of data on many of Jellinek's symptoms require skills beyond those acquired in training as a cultural anthropologist. It probably is no accident that the best data we have on the incidence of, for example, cirrhosis in Indian groups are provided by an interdisciplinary team (i.e., Levy and Kunitz). Alcohol studies need anthropological perspective, but obviously they require other skills as well. Collaboration probably is the best approach, when it can be arranged.

28. *Decrease of Sexual Drive:* INSUFFICIENT EVIDENCE

Jellinek (81, *p. 681*) wrote that a decrease in sexual drive is one of the frequent organic effects of alcohol addiction.

[93]E.g., Brenner (15); Jellinek (83); Keller (91); Popham (158); Seeley (171).

[94]Keller, M. Personal communication, 15 March 1972.

Accounts of sexual activity, including sexual aggression, among Indians under the influence of alcohol[95] tempt one to entertain the notion that alcohol has the opposite effect in this group. However, it is seldom clear whether the protagonists of these episodes are frequent heavy drinkers or not. Among the Navaho, Levy et al. (115, *p. 138*) and Levy (110, *p. 317*) report that sexual jealousy is one of the dominant motives for criminal homicide and the suspected wife or her lover is the victim significantly more often than in comparison groups, but jealousy is not necessarily correlated with sexual drive.

The correlation between levels of alcohol intake and sexual drive has not been systematically investigated, particularly among Indians. Devising standards for "normal" and "decreased" sexual drive would no doubt pose difficult problems, as would data collection; these obstacles may account in part for the dearth of evidence on this symptom.

29. Alcoholic Jealousy: INSUFFICIENT EVIDENCE

The decrease in sexual drive discussed above is supposed to increase "hostility towards the wife and is rationalized into her extramarital sex activities, which gives rise to the well-known *alcoholic jealousy*" (81, *p. 681*).

The Honigmanns (68, *p. 600*), reporting a high rate of drunken aggression against wives among the Kaska, comment that this behavior repeats "the universally familiar pattern of jealousy accentuated by alcohol." On the other hand, Devereux (33, *p. 218, footnote*) insists that jealousy is not a universal response: "One cannot help being amazed by the tenacity with which modern psychologists . . . cling to the view that jealousy is a natural and innate sentiment, in the face of contradictory evidence furnished not merely by anthropologists and historians but even by students of primate zoology. *Homines id quod volunt credunt!*"

From the accounts so far available, it seems likely that sexual jealousy may be prevalent[96] in some Indian groups but rare in others (e.g., 33, *p. 218;* 175, *p. 14*). Investigations would have to control for this variable before the occurrence among Indians of alcoholic

[95]Devereux (33, *p. 213*); Heath (62, *p. 18*); Horton (71, *p. 251*) [Papago]; Lemert (107, *p. 341*).

[96]E.g., Hamer (58, *p. 293*); Honigmann and Honigmann (68, *p. 600;* 70, *p. 75*); Levy (110, *p. 315*); Levy et al. (115, *p. 138*).

jealousy could be evaluated. Thus far data which would have a bearing on this symptom are extremely scarce.

30. Regular Matutinal Drinking: INSUFFICIENT EVIDENCE

Jellinek (81, *pp. 681, 682*) describes morning drinking as follows:

"By this time remorse, resentment, struggle between alcoholic needs and duties, loss of self-esteem, and doubts and false reassurance have so disorganized the addict that he cannot start the day without steadying himself with alcohol immediately after arising or even before getting out of bed. This is the beginning of *regular matutinal drinking* . . . which previously had occurred on rare occasions only. . . . 'Morning drink' jeopardizes his effort to comply with his vocational duties as this effort involves a conscious resistance against apparent or real 'physical demand' for alcohol."

This description would seem to exclude social morning drinking, such as that associated with binges. As Kunitz has pointed out,[97] since by definition binge drinking continues around the clock and binges are reported to be the characteristic drinking style among most of the Indian groups covered here, morning drinking must be common among them, too. But the type of morning drinking associated with binges does not necessarily fit Jellinek's descriptions.

Only a few observers explicitly mention morning drinking among Indians.[98] These accounts appear to me to refer to the solitary pattern Jellinek had in mind, rather than the more social type associated with binges among Indians. The relative difficulty of detecting such private behavior makes these reports noteworthy, but there are too few to justify rating the symptom as present.

The notion that morning drinking is a major symptom of alcohol addiction (78, *p. 47*) no doubt stems in part from dominant-society job- and time-centered viewpoints. If Indians do not share these attitudes, a powerful deterrent to morning drinking would seem to be absent among them, and interpretation of such behavior as evidence of alcohol addiction would be open to question.

31. Prolonged Intoxications: PRESENT

Jellinek (81, *p. 682*) says that prolonged intoxications mark the beginning of the chronic phase of alcohol addiction (see Table 1 for the phases). He comments:

[97]Kunitz, S. J. Personal communication, 25 May 1971.
[98]Ferguson (46, *p. 95*); Jessor (86, *p. 69*); Slater (239, *p. 21*); Whittaker (212, *p. 475*).

"The increasingly dominating role of alcohol, and the struggle against the 'demand' set up by matutinal drinking, at last break down the resistance of the addict and he finds himself for the first time intoxicated in the daytime and on a weekday and continues in that state for several days until he is entirely incapacitated. This is the onset of *prolonged intoxications* . . . referred to in the vernacular as 'benders'."

How does the behavior described above differ from loss of control (Symptom 8)? Jellinek limited the scope of that concept to inability to control the quantity consumed, and hence the duration of a bout. The introduction of prolonged intoxications as a separate symptom implies that Jellinek considered the behavior thus described to be somehow different from loss of control. It is possible that Jellinek meant to confine loss of control to the inability to interrupt a bout before intoxication occurred; but if that inability lasted longer than a day, this constituted a separate symptom of alcohol addiction—prolonged intoxications. The theoretical justification for such a distinction is unclear. In any case, the distinction is unnecessary under Keller's broad formulation of loss of control (94) which has been used herein; that is, the inability to consistently choose "whether he shall drink, and if he drinks . . . whether he shall stop," of which prolonged intoxications would be one of several possible manifestations, depending on circumstances.

Since, according to this definition, prolonged intoxications are a special case of loss of control (i.e., manifestation *b*, inability to control the quantity consumed and hence the duration of a bout) the evidence of their occurrence among Indians was documented under that symptom. The occurrence of prolonged intoxications has been reported in 23 "accounts" covering 8 different culture areas and all 3 community types distinguished herein (Table 2 and Appendix).[99]

This evidence presents a dilemma. Loss of control was rated IN-SUFFICIENT EVIDENCE because, in all but a few accounts, it was unclear whether control was lost or simply absent among Indians. Since we have considered prolonged intoxications as a manifestation of loss of control, and it is unclear from the available evidence whether the protagonists cannot or simply do not avoid prolonged intoxications,

---

[99]Footnotes 22, 23 and 30 plus the text discussion of binges contain 28 citations indicating that Prolonged intoxications (Symptom 31) are PRESENT in the groups covered. Of these, 23 qualify as "accounts": (10), (16), (22 and 23), (25), (27), (38), (40), (46 and 48), (52), (58), (74), (97), (99), (101, 111 and 112), (107 and 108), (162), (168), (169), (175), (187), 212), (230), (232).

it would seem to follow that this symptom should be rated similarly. However, Jellinek separated prolonged intoxications from loss of control and thus seemed to elevate the behavior to the status of an independent symptom of alcohol addiction, with or without the co-occurrence of loss of control. Under these circumstances, since it is clear that prolonged intoxications do occur among Indians, the symptom has been rated PRESENT.

32. Marked Ethical Deterioration: INSUFFICIENT EVIDENCE

Standards of correct behavior are no doubt a cross-cultural universal. I will ignore the problems raised by Jellinek's term "ethical," with its strong overtones of dominant-society assumptions about a "moral" basis for such standards, and assume that he merely refers to behavior which a group strongly disapproves. The fact that different behavior is condemned by different groups would not in itself inhibit interpreting as symptomatic of alcohol addiction behavior which, deviant in the group's own terms, is clearly aggravated by drinking. Thus, even though Indians may think alcohol absolves the drinker of responsibility for his actions, if he commits acts as a result of his drinking, which are defined as deviant by his group, this would qualify as evidence of the occurrence of alcohol-induced marked ethical deterioration.

The qualifying statements above suggest one of the problems in interpreting such behavior as a sign of alcohol addiction. Although deviant behavior and drinking may have a high incidence in a particular group, and even in a particular individual, the correlation may well be fortuitous, as Levy and Kunitz (113, p. 227) and also Levy et al. (115, p. 133) concluded in the case of homicide among the Navaho.

The data available so far on Indian drinking are inadequate for rating the occurrence of this symptom. Evidence on the incidence of behavior defined as deviant by Indians is often difficult to separate from reports of acts judged deviant by dominant-society standards, and the role of alcohol in the occurrence of such behavior is unclear.

33. Impairment of Thinking: INSUFFICIENT EVIDENCE

This symptom is described by Jellinek (81, p. 682) in the context of the chronic phase of alcohol addiction. His only elaboration is the remark that the impairment is "not irreversible." From this I infer that he was not referring to long-range effects of the magnitude of brain damage but rather to decrements immediately after intake. The literature on the effects of alcohol on thinking processes as summarized by Wallgren and Barry (206, *pp. 331–343*) indicates that verbal performance, problem solving, learning and memory all are sensitive to the effects of alcohol in the populations studied. Jellinek does not indicate how he measured this symptom in the population used to establish the norms; he may have relied on subjective impressions.

The literature on Indian drinking includes no accounts of systematic attempts to measure impairment of thinking in that group. In fact, it contains no allusions to "impressions" of the occurrence of this symptom. The design of experiments to measure alcohol-induced thinking decrements among Indians would present the usual challenge of cross-cultural psychological testing, and has not been attempted so far. The symptom is therefore rated INSUFFICIENT EVIDENCE.

34. *Alcoholic Psychoses:* INSUFFICIENT EVIDENCE

This term covers several phenomena usually identified by separate terms, including delirium tremens, alcoholic hallucinosis and Korsakoff's psychosis (recent memory failure). Delirium tremens is itself a composite. The basis for distinguishing some of its components from each other and from other symptoms is not obvious to nonspecialists—for example, delirium versus hallucinations, tremens versus "tremors" (Symptom 39), or the panic exhibited during delirium tremens versus "indefinable fears" (Symptom 38).

Keller[100] believes the conceptual distinctions among the components of alcoholic psychoses are clear enough, if the diagnostician is alert to them, but he notes that many physicians are not. Kunitz et al. (101, *p. 682*) seem to acknowledge that the diagnosis of alcoholic psychoses is beyond the skill of nonspecialists when they warn that diagnoses made before psychiatric diagnostic facilities were readily available on the Navaho reservation are suspect. Such facilities probably are still unavailable on many reservations. Thus, it would seem that hospital records do not necessarily provide an accurate source of data on the incidence of such disorders as delirium tremens. Furthermore, even if diagnoses were completely reliable, comparison of medical records on Indians with those on the general population may

---

[100]Keller, M. Personal communication, 15 March 1972.

not provide a valid indication of relative incidence of alcoholic psychoses (or cirrhosis and other disorders, for that matter). A higher proportion of total cases may be reflected in records of Indians than of Whites because treatment is free. A lower proportion of cases may be recorded because treatment facilities are often far away and because some Indians may believe that witchcraft or other causes outside the province of medicine are responsible for the symptoms.

In addition, alcoholic psychoses occur in not more than 10% of all alcohol addicts (81, *p. 682*). Therefore, given the relatively small size of the Indian population, absence of these manifestations in this group might be accounted for by chance. Even the undisputed presence of alcoholic psychoses among Indians might not be a reliable indicator of the presence of addiction, since the binge drinking style which apparently predominates among them is said to be more likely than other styles to produce the symptom (101, *p. 682*).

Despite Keller's conviction that diagnostic training is the key to more reliable data on these phenomena, it seems possible that clarification of the semantics of "alcoholic psychoses" might also aid this effort.

The difficulties outlined above may partly explain the dearth of evidence on the occurrence of alcoholic psychoses among Indians. Nevertheless, there are a few studies which indicate that delirium tremens[101] and alcoholic hallucinosis[102] may or do occur among Indians. Unfortunately, the majority of these works cover the Navaho only. Few reports attempt to estimate the incidence of these phenomena among the Indians and in the general population. Levy and Kunitz provide one noteworthy exception (113, *p. 233*). In their sample of Navaho and Hopi who scored in the "alcoholic" range on the Preoccupation-with-Alcohol Scale, nearly half reported delirium tremens or alcoholic hallucinosis or both. Among Whites and Negroes hospitalized for alcoholic complaints, only 25% reported these symptoms.

Approximately one-third of Slater's (239, *p. 20*) sample of Uintah-

[101]Berreman (10, *p. 511*); Ferguson (47, *p. 162*); IHS Task Force on Alcoholism (75, *p. 10*); LaBarre 104, *p. 43* [single case]; Lemert (107, *pp. 359, 363; 108, pp. 103, 106*); Levy and Kunitz (113, *p. 233*); Martinez (127, *p. 3*); Sievers (174, *p. 77*); Slater (239, *p. 20*); Whittaker (212, *p. 476*).

[102]Boyer (14, *pp. 217, 218*); Koolage (99, *p. 102*); Lemert (107, *p. 358*); Levy and Kunitz (113, *p. 233*). The IHS Task Force warns physicians to look for this symptom, so they apparently expect it to occur among Indians (76, *p. 3*).

Ouray arrested for drunkenness reported having experienced delirium tremens, a rate much closer to that of the general population than the Navaho–Hopi rate reported by Levy and Kunitz, but this difference might reflect differing criteria for inclusion in the sample and methods of data gathering rather than variation between the tribes in question.

Slater asked the following question: "Have you ever had the D.T.'s —seen things or heard things that were not real?" This unfortunate wording brings to mind another pitfall in interpreting delirium and hallucinations as evidence of alcohol addiction among Indians. Are they culturally predisposed to hallucinate? Levy and Kunitz (113, *p. 233*) dropped this possibility from consideration because traditional symbols did not figure prominently in the accounts of hallucinations by Navaho, and because alcohol-associated hallucinations were reported by the Hopi despite their traditional opposition to visions and individual power experiences. Nevertheless, it seems to me that cross-cultural differences and similarities in the manifestations of alcoholic hallucinations and delirium tremens deserve further investigation.

35. Drinks with Persons Far Below His Social Level: INSUFFICIENT EVIDENCE.

Concerning this symptom, Jellinek (81, *p. 682*) says: "The loss of morale is so heightened that the addict *drinks with persons far below his social level* ... in preference to his usual associates—perhaps as an opportunity to appear superior. ..." Several characteristics of drinking behavior which already have been documented among the Indian groups covered herein might seem to preclude the occurrence of this symptom. For example, if the drinker does not feel guilty about drinking, and he is not rejected by his peers, he would have no incentive for drinking with persons of lower status. Nevertheless, for reasons already discussed, I will refrain from basing a rating on this inference. However, if status distinctions are less sharp in the Indian groups observed than in the dominant society (whether reflecting egalitarian values from earlier times, the realities of present-day economic conditions, or other causes) this symptom might occur but escape detection because it would be relatively difficult to observe. In any case, the evidence provided in the literature so far does not justify rating the occurrence of this symptom.

36. *Recourse to "Technical Products":* INSUFFICIENT EVIDENCE

In the general adult population, the practice of drinking alcohol substitutes is probably as much an index of poverty as of addiction. Although perhaps only addicts use "technical products," such as shaving lotion, most addicts do not. Among the age group which cannot legally purchase customary beverages, the inference of addiction from this practice is of course uncertain. In a similar manner, among Indians, circumstances (such as remoteness from supply and prohibition) make problematic the connection between the use of alcohol substitutes and addiction.

Five authors mention use of alcohol substitutes by Indians. Among the Eskimo of Aklavik, Clairmont (22, *p. 3; 23, p. 55*) makes it clear that the reported drinking of perfume, wood alcohol and shaving lotion is a last resort, when the drinker has no other choice (until recently, because liquor privileges were denied to natives, and subsequently, because the nearest source is several hours away by boat and a half hour by plane). A more usual substitute is home brew, but the maturation of a batch does not always coincide with the urge for a party. Von Hentig (66, *p. 79*), apparently in this instance referring to Indians in seven northern states, says: "If liquor is not available they drink canned heat, rubbing alcohol or hair tonic. Some Indians will drain and drink the contents of auto radiators. In one case three Indian boys died from drinking Prestone." These data came from a 1934 government report and, thus, pertain to the period when prohibition applied to Indians only, not to the general population.

The Honigmanns (68, *p. 578*) imply that the Kaska of "Delio" drink after-shave lotions and lemon extract but this, too, occurred during a period when Indians could not legally drink, in a place where even Whites were regulated by rationing and the nearest source of supply was several hundred miles away (*pp. 585–586*). Home brew was the preferred alternative.

An account by Hurt and Brown (74, *p. 224*) of the Dakota Sioux drinking alcohol substitutes refers to the early reservation period, and thus is not considered in the rating of symptoms.

Lemert (108, *pp. 98, 99*) quotes a Homalthko as saying, contemptuously, "I don't drink home-brew, vanilla extract, hair tonic, shaving lotion, perfume or Listerine like some guys do. I buy whisky and I have my ways of getting it." Thus, these practices obviously occur, but again in the context of prohibition and isolation from a source of supply. In another work, Lemert refers to the use of alcohol substitutes among Northwest Coast Indians in the early historical period (107, *pp. 307, 340*) and in modern times among adolescents (*p. 353*). Historical accounts are excluded from the ratings (in any case, the beverages appear to have been sold to the Indians as legitimate liquor). In adolescents the use of technical products does not necessarily imply addiction, as mentioned earlier.

I have encountered no firm data on the incidence of the use of technical products in the general adult population. Even if we had such information, to provide a fair comparison the practice among Indians would have to occur in postprohibition times, and in a setting where isolation from supply was not greater than in the comparison group. I have found no such account in the literature.

Even if it were firmly established that the incidence of this practice is as high among Indians as in the general population, or higher, the relative rate of poverty among Indians would have to be taken into account in these comparisons, since economic necessity is doubtless another element in the occurrence of this behavior. In other words, the comparisons of incidence should be between the populations at risk, i.e., poverty stricken folk in both populations, with adjustments for the high proportion of total Indian population with low incomes.

37. *Loss of Alcohol Tolerance:* INSUFFICIENT EVIDENCE

Jellinek (81, *p. 682*) says that the occurrence of this symptom is indicated when "Half of the previously required amount of alcohol may be sufficient to bring about a stuporous state." In their two-volume review of the alcohol literature, Wallgren and Barry (206, *pp. 497–499*) summarize evidence which they believe demonstrates the development of increased tolerance to alcohol in humans after prolonged exposure to alcohol. As far as I can tell, they present no evidence to substantiate the opposite effect. Jellinek (81) does not tell us his basis for including loss of tolerance to alcohol as a symptom of alcohol addiction; apparently this experience was reported by a number of alcoholics.

It seems to be difficult to rule out factors other than alcohol, such as brain damage from blows or falls, as the cause of loss of tolerance to alcohol, if it does indeed occur. Nevertheless, Keller points out,[103] such brain damage (presumably only in association with other symp-

[103]Keller, M. Personal communication, 15 March 1972.

toms) could serve as indirect presumptive evidence of alcoholism, since alcoholics are far more likely than others to experience it.

Assuming that loss of tolerance to alcohol actually does occur among alcohol addicts, for whatever reason, there are several obstacles to investigation of this phenomenon among Indians. For one thing, it is difficult to determine the actual alcohol intake "When a bottle is being passed around and glasses are not used and when the alcohol content varies," as seems to be the custom in some Indian groups (113, *p. 229*). Even if intake were known, measuring the effects is difficult, and the task is complicated by temporal variations in the tolerance of any one individual, by variations in tolerance among individuals, and by the suspected Indian practice of feigning intoxication, already discussed.

So far we have no data on which to rate the occurrence of this symptom among Indian groups.

38. Indefinable Fears: INSUFFICIENT EVIDENCE

Indefinable fears may also occur in the earlier "crucial" phase of alcohol addiction but in the "chronic" phase they may become "persistent," according to Jellinek (81, *p. 682*).

I have encountered no evidence relative to the occurrence of this symptom among Indians.

39. Tremors: INSUFFICIENT EVIDENCE

Tremors may occur in the earlier "crucial" phase of alcohol addiction, but in the chronic phase, Jellinek says, they are "present as soon as alcohol disappears from the organism. In consequence the addict 'controls' the symptoms through alcohol" (81, *p. 683*).

If alcohol addiction could be inferred from the mere occurrence of tremors, or even from the practice of "having some of the hair of the dog that bit you" to control the tremors, our estimates of the incidence of addiction in the general population would no doubt have to be revised sharply upward. It probably has become obvious that the manifestation of one symptom, alone, does not make an addict in Jellinek's terms; the constellation he requires for this diagnosis will be presented later. In the meantime, each of Jellinek's symptoms is treated as an independent phenomenon for the purpose of rating its occurrence among Indians.

Levy and Kunitz report (113, *p. 233*) that 60% of all the Navaho and Hopi drinkers who scored in the "alcoholic" range on the Preoccupation with Alcohol Scale said they experienced bouts of tremulousness after drinking stopped. At first glance this statistic would seem to warrant rating tremors as present in this group. However, Levy and Kunitz argue convincingly that this incidence of tremors does not necessarily indicate a high rate of alcohol addiction. Noting recent research which indicates that serious withdrawal symptoms are most likely to occur when drinking ceases rapidly and completely, they postulate that the high rate of tremors results from circumstances which lead Indians to sudden cessation of alcohol intake—arrest, unconsciousness (in turn encouraged by the rapid drinking style), and remoteness from supply (resulting from tribal prohibition, for example). They say (113, *p. 233*): "Once tremulousness starts, there is no alcohol available for tapering off, as it is for the majority of Skid Row drinkers and White drinkers in general." Thus, the comparative incidence of tremors and other withdrawal symptoms in different societies cannot be taken "as a firm measure of the differences in the level of alcoholism in these populations. It would appear that even these physiological manifestations are to a large extent determined by the style of drinking which is in turn culturally determined."

In any case, no conclusions about the incidence of "tremors" among Indians, as defined herein, can be drawn from evidence on only two groups. Although we may eventually find that tremors occur at a high rate in many Indian groups, the influence of drinking style suggests caution in interpreting such evidence as a sign of alcohol addiction among them. Levy and Kunitz (113, *p. 233*) warn: "Thus, while it is obvious that these people drink sufficiently to experience withdrawal symptoms and may, by this criterion, be safely labeled as alcoholic, it is not clear that the nature of their addiction, if that is what it is, is the same as what is found in our own population."

40. Psychomotor Inhibition: INSUFFICIENT EVIDENCE

Jellinek (81, *p. 683*) describes psychomotor inhibition as "the inability to initiate a simple mechanical act—such as winding a watch —in the absence of alcohol." The addict uses alcohol to "control" psychomotor inhibition, as in the case of tremors, discussed above.

I have encountered no data on the occurrence of this symptom among Indians.

41. Drinking Takes on an Obsessive Character: INSUFFICIENT EVIDENCE

Whatever the needs which originally motivated drinking, at this point they are exceeded by the need to control tremors and psycho-motor inhibition, and the drinking takes on an obsessive character, according to Jellinek (81, *p. 683*). Jellinek does not detail how "ob-sessive" drinking is recognized or measured, or how it is distinguished from some other symptoms, such as, "preoccupation with alcohol" (Symptom 3), "avid drinking" (Symptom 4) or "behavior becomes alcohol centered" (Symptom 18).

It is difficult to interpret the available evidence which seems per-tinent to this point. Such phrases as "desperation about the desire for alcohol" (58, *p. 289*), "sense of urgency . . . to continue until he is totally inebriated" (165, *p. 47*) and "uncontrollable impulses to drink" (212, *p. 475*), used to describe drinking by Indians, all seem to suggest the possibility of "obsessive" drinking in the groups de-scribed.

On the other hand, although Lemert (108, *p. 96*) remarks on the "compulsive nature" of the need for alcohol once the Indians have become drunk, he doubts (107, *p. 362; 108, p. 106*) that alcohol ad-diction is present in the Northwest Coast Indians. Berreman (10, *p. 511*) denies the existence of "compulsive or addictive drinking" among an Aleut group. Dailey (28, *p. 26*) says that Indians are not "gripped with that iron-willed compulsion to seek alcohol in ways characteristic of alcoholics in our society." If the quoted phrases clearly referred to the same thing, and this "thing" obviously quali-fied as "obsessive" drinking in Jellinek's terms, a rating of CONFLICT-ING EVIDENCE probably would have been assigned to this symptom. However, their equivalency to each other and to Jellinek's intent is not certain. I have chosen to judge the evidence insufficient to merit rating the occurrence of this symptom.

42. Vague Religious Desires Develop: INSUFFICIENT EVIDENCE

Jellinek (81, *p. 683*) reports that vague religious desires develop in approximately 60% of addicts "as the rationalizations become weaker." It is clear that reactions against alcohol have figured prom-inently in several religion-oriented nativistic movements,[104] and also have stimulated Indian participation in Christian sects (e.g., 107, *p. 367*). However, it is not possible to justify a conclusion that the religious desires reflected in these movements are symptomatic of alcohol addiction.

There is little direct evidence bearing on the occurrence of this

[104]For example, the Handsome Lake movement, the Native American Church, and the Ghost Dance. Dozier (36, *p. 81*) discusses this point.

phenomenon among Indians. In a Uintah-Ouray sample of people arrested for alcohol-related offenses, Slater reports (239, *p. 18*) that 20% chose "help from a religious leader" from a list of possible sources of help in stopping drinking. Alcoholics Anonymous, which contains a religious element, also received a high score (29%). But of course this cannot be interpreted as evidence that this proportion of the group were demonstrating a symptom of alcohol addiction, particularly since the question was worded in such a way that "It is not known whether they felt a need for help themselves or were simply indicating the type of help they felt would be most acceptable to the Indian people in general" (239, *p. 18*). Slater's data are about the only evidence available which seem even slightly pertinent in assessing the occurrence of vague religious desires associated with drinking among Indians. This symptom would seem to present particularly difficult data collection problems.

43. Rationalization System Fails: INSUFFICIENT EVIDENCE

Jellinek (81, *p. 683*) says: "Finally, in the course of the frequently prolonged intoxications, the rationalizations become so frequent and so mercilessly tested against reality that the entire *rationalization system fails* . . . and the addict admits defeat. He now becomes spontaneously accessible to treatment."

If rationalization of drinking behavior (Symptom 9) were rare among Indians, we might expect failure of such a system to be even more uncommon in the groups covered. However, the evidence has been judged insufficient to rate "rationalize drinking behavior," and is even less adequate for rating "rationalization system fails."

"Defeat" is apparently a crucial element in Jellinek's description. He remarks (81, *p. 683*): "Formerly it was thought that the addict must reach this stage of utter defeat in order to be treated successfully. Clinical experience has shown, however, that this 'defeat' can be induced long before it would occur of itself. . . ."

If failure of a rationalization system is really the crucial condition for treatment of alcohol addiction, proponents of the reverse-firewater hypothesis might well want to investigate in more detail whether or not Indians do rationalize their drinking behavior. If not, it might be postulated that the absence of rationalizations about drinking behavior could be a crucial variable in explaining the alleged absence or rarity of alcohol addiction among Indians.

This leads back to the original question. Is alcohol addiction rare among Indians?

5

Summary Tally of the
Symptom Ratings

IN Chapter 4, 44 symptoms of alcohol addiction were rated as PRESENT, ABSENT-RARE, CONFLICTING EVIDENCE, or INSUFFICIENT EVIDENCE on the basis of data culled from the literature on Indian drinking. In the present chapter the individual symptom ratings will be combined to see whether they confirm or deny the reverse-firewater hypothesis that alcohol addiction is rare among Indians. As shown in Table 1, only 2 symptoms of alcohol addiction were rated ABSENT-RARE, and only 3 were rated PRESENT. On 39 of the symptoms (91%), the evidence was judged to be too CONFLICTING (3 symptoms) or INSUFFICIENT[1] (36 symptoms) to justify the conclusion that they do or do not occur among the Indian groups covered.

Thus, if numbers of symptoms alone were the sole criterion, the conclusion that the evidence neither supports nor confirms the reverse-firewater hypothesis would be unavoidable. If more observations on more symptoms were available, the balance could go either way.

However, as seems clear from the discussion thus far, some of the symptoms may well be more important than others in diagnosing alcohol addiction. For example, the progression implied by the labels of the phases into which Jellinek grouped the symptoms (prodromal, crucial and chronic) suggests that the more advanced the phase in which a symptom occurs, the more significant it is as an indicator of addiction. But, the details of the phases and the sequence of symptoms are not sufficiently accepted—see, e.g., Trice and Wahl (194)—to warrant basing a weighting system thereon. In any case, the symptoms rated PRESENT are evenly distributed among the three phases; those rated ABSENT-RARE occur in the first two phases.

---

[1]Of course, the rating INSUFFICIENT is relative; by usual anthropological standards, even the evidence provided in the literature on the five symptoms rated PRESENT or ABSENT–RARE is subject to some of the criticisms discussed under Method, Chapter 3.

Jellinek specifically acknowledged differential weight among the symptoms in the following description of what he considered the most reliable bases for identifying nonaddicted drinkers (81, *p. 684*): "after 10 or 12 years of heavy drinking without 'loss of control' *[8]*, while symptoms 2 [surreptitious drinking] 6 [avoid reference to alcohol] were persistent and 'palimpsests' [*1* and *7*] were rare and did not occur after medium alcohol intake, the differential diagnosis is rather safe."[2]

However, even if evaluation of the reverse-firewater hypothesis were limited to the five symptoms Jellinek appears to consider most vital, the picture is no more clear. The evidence in the literature on drinking by Indians has been judged insufficient to warrant a rating for any of these.

The apparent association between some of the symptoms poses other weighting problems. For example, a negative rating for at least 8 symptoms (*2, 9, 13, 16, 21, 23, 35,* and *43*), and perhaps a few others (e.g., *20* and *24*), might seem to follow logically from the reported absence of guilt (Symptom 5) and its corollary (107, *p. 365*), the lack of social sanctions against drinking (see the discussion of Symptom 10). If these 10 symptoms had been rated on the basis of inference from the absence of guilt and sanctions, the tally totals would have been altered somewhat, PRESENT 3, ABSENT–RARE 12, CONFLICTING EVIDENCE 2; but a majority, 27, would still be rated INSUFFICIENT EVIDENCE.

As has been frequently mentioned, however, the inference of the absence of other symptoms from the apparent absence of guilt and social sanctions against drinking is fraught with ethnocentric pitfalls. Guilt and rejection might be sufficient but not necessary preconditions for symptoms. As already pointed out, distinct phenomena, such as pride (which would not appear to be rare among Indians), could also be implicated.

If sufficient direct evidence were available to rate the symptoms whose absence might be considered to follow from the absence of Symptoms 5 and 10, the apparent interdependence among them does not mean they could automatically be reduced to a weight of 1 in evaluating the reverse-firewater hypothesis. If the notion were accepted that alcohol addiction is at least partly culturally determined (as well as defined), it is of course possible that a single value or

[2]Bracketed material has been inserted to facilitate reference to the numbers and labels of symptoms in Table 1.

complex of values in a culture could account for the absence of alcohol addiction and hence for the absence of all its symptoms in the group. Nevertheless, one has the uncomfortable feeling that guilt and sanctions may be unduly emphasized in Jellinek's list, since the evidence in the literature on American Indian drinking suggests that these symptoms are perhaps culture specific.

A similar constellation centered on binge drinking also illustrates the general problem of weighting. As Kunitz has pointed out,[3] the occurrence of avid drinking (Symptom 4), morning drinking (Symptom 30) and prolonged intoxications (Symptom 31) follows, by definition, from the apparent prevalence among Indians of binge drinking. Furthermore, Kunitz says, blackouts (Symptoms 1 and 7) and withdrawal symptoms (e.g., Symptom 39) are the almost inevitable result of the binge drinking style.[4] In addition, according to Kunitz, loss of control (Symptom 8) can be judged present only in the context of the binge. There also may be a positive correlation between binge-style drinking and Symptom 34, alcoholic psychoses (101, p. 682).

If these associated symptoms all occurred simply as the inevitable result of the group's usual drinking style, rather than as a reflection of individual motivation, the high incidence of binge drinking among Indians could unduly influence the number of symptoms of alcohol addiction which might be rated as PRESENT if we had sufficient data to rate these symptoms.

On the other hand, Levy and Kunitz (113, p. 232) suggest a possible negative correlation between cirrhosis and periodic binges. The latter "may allow for an adequate diet during periods of sobriety and in this manner protect the drinker from contraction of the disease. It is also possible, however, that the relative inaccessibility of alcohol in many areas also may protect against cirrhosis." If so, the predominance of binge drinking among Indians might tend to minimize the incidence of this relatively objective symptom among them and thus might even lead to underestimation of their addiction rate.

A case could be made for evaluating the reverse-firewater hypothesis solely on the occurrence of loss of control (Symptom 8). Jellinek (81, p. 674) considered his version of that concept as the critical diagnostic sign, and the author of the expanded interpretation of loss of control used herein (94, p. 153) calls it the pathognomonic

[3]Kunitz, S. J. Personal communication, 25 May 1971.
[4]See also Kunitz et al. (101, p. 682).

symptom of alcohol addiction. Even this approach, however, would not allow a clear decision one way or the other. The present literature does not even unequivocally indicate that a high proportion of Indians cannot control their drinking, much less that they have lost such control. In a minority group, whose notions of "acceptable" behavior may differ greatly from those of the general population, the whole question of the appropriateness of the practice of inferring loss of control and, hence, alcohol addiction, from failure to meet dominant-society standards of "prudence" requires a great deal more scrutiny, particularly in the perspective of Bacon's (4) elaboration of the loss-of-control concept.

Another possible approach to weighting symptoms is suggested by Levy and Kunitz (113, *p. 234*). They categorize manifestations of excessive drinking as "physiological" vs "behavioral." In context, these observers seem to imply that the former deserve relatively greater weight than the latter as indicators of alcohol addiction in a minority group, because they are relatively more culture free, though not entirely so.

I will explore the possibility of devising a weighting scheme along these lines. For this purpose, I will consider only the five symptoms for which the available literature provides sufficient data to justify a definite rating of PRESENT or ABSENT–RARE according to the criteria used herein. Of these five symptoms, only one—Symptom 27, hospitalization: alcoholic cirrhosis—seems to qualify as a physiological manifestation. It is rated PRESENT. Of the other four, all behavioral, two (Symptoms 4, avid drinking, and 31, prolonged intoxications) are rated PRESENT and two (Symptoms 5, guilt feelings, and 10, social pressures countered) are rated ABSENT–RARE. Even if physiological manifestations deserve more weight than behavioral ones in evaluating the reverse-firewater hypothesis, should the apparent presence of alcoholic cirrhosis be the deciding variable, outweighing the two symptoms rated ABSENT–RARE? The numbers involved are so low that the question seems absurd.

However, if the evidence merited ratings for more symptoms, the question could become interesting. What if, for example, it were agreed that in addition to Symptom 27 (hospitalization: cirrhosis), Symptoms 34 (alcoholic psychoses), 39 (tremors) and 40 (psychomotor inhibition) should be categorized as "physiological" and also merited the rating PRESENT on the basis of the literature? In the meantime, suppose the remaining 40 symptoms (which for the sake of argument would be categorized as behavioral) were rated

ABSENT–RARE? Then what would be the verdict about the validity of the reverse-firewater hypothesis?

The question is particularly difficult to answer since, as Levy and Kunitz have shown, even the "physiological" symptoms are at least partly culturally determined. Yet "physiological" symptoms would seem to be relatively more objective indicators of alcohol addiction than "behavioral" symptoms, and thus would seem to deserve more weight in evaluating the reverse-firewater hypothesis. On the other hand, Keller (92, *p. 29*), who labels alcoholism a "psychological disablement," thinks that many physicians have been indoctrinated with the pharmacological notion of physical addiction and with the distinction between psychological and physiological addiction, although there is no way of telling them apart. He writes, "The evidence for physiological addiction has never been produced. The evidence for altered cell metabolism has not been produced." And he quotes "a tough-minded pharmacologist," M. H. Seevers, as calling the notions of altered cell metabolism and physical dependence "exercises in semantics, or plain flights of the imagination."

In view of the fundamental disagreement in the alcohol literature about the relative importance of physical versus behavioral symptoms in the diagnosis of alcohol addiction, I will not propose a weighting system along these lines. The foregoing discussion is included merely to pinpoint some of the problems for the person who attempts the task.

Another complication related to weighting also stems from my system for rating symptoms. As mentioned in Chapter 3, the weight of evidence is uneven among the rated symptoms. For the 5 symptoms rated PRESENT or ABSENT–RARE (Table 2), the number of supporting citations varies as follows: *4*, avid drinking, 16; *5*, guilt feelings about drinking behavior, 17; *10*, social pressures (countered), 34; *27*, hospitalization (cirrhosis), 8; *31*, prolonged intoxications, 23. As explained under the discussion thereof, Symptom 27 was rated PRESENT despite the small number of citations because one of these, from an authoritative source (198), reported a cirrhosis death rate for all Indians in the U.S.A. nearly double the rate in the general population. The citations supporting Symptom *10* are the most numerous, 34, but even these represent only about a third of the total works cited in support of ratings. Thus, if evidence on the occurrence of the 5 symptoms were available for more groups, the ratings might be reversed.

The rating system employed herein leads to a related problem. Symptom X may be rated PRESENT in a large number of the Indian groups covered. Symptom Y may be rated PRESENT in an equally large but different set of the groups. The chart then would indicate that Symptoms X and Y are PRESENT among Indians, as defined herein. This, of course, tends to disguise data which are of potentially great interest. To facilitate comparison of the distribution of symptoms, Table 2 shows the Indian groups, by culture area, in which the five symptoms for which evidence merited a definite rating were judged to be PRESENT or ABSENT–RARE.

At first glance, the apparent consistency in symptom ratings in Table 2 seems striking. That is, Symptoms 4, 27 and 31 are rated PRESENT and Symptoms 5 and 10 are rated ABSENT in every group for which sufficient evidence was available to justify a rating. However, this apparent homogeneity is partly an artifact of the rating criteria; i.e., near-unanimity among the observers who mention a symptom, and, in the absence of data on incidence, rating on the basis of occurrence alone.

More significant, the summary does not suggest complementary distribution of the five symptoms among Indian groups or culture areas. This seems to suggest that cultural differences among tribes do not account for variation in the occurrence of the different symptoms. However, this too is probably merely a reflection of the inadequacy of the data on which the ratings are based. In the rare cases in which careful comparisons have been made among tribes (e.g., 112, 113), the evidence strongly suggests that cultural differences among Indian groups do indeed correlate with differences in occurrence of some of the symptoms. Furthermore, when observers have specifically looked for variations in the incidence of symptoms within subgroups of a tribe, as Levy and Kunitz have for cirrhosis among the Navaho and Hopi (112, 113), such variation has been found.

Exploration of detailed differences in the distribution of symptoms within and among Indian groups must await the availability of more data comparable to that of Levy and Kunitz. The evidence offered in the literature so far is generally inadequate to support refined comparisons, yet these could significantly advance our understanding of the dynamics of Indian drinking and perhaps of the concept of alcohol addiction as well.

If there is any complementary distribution among tribes or culture

CHART 2.—*"Solitary Drinking"* CONFLICTING EVIDENCE

	PRESENT	ABSENT—RARE
Arctic Coast	Aleut of Aklavik (22, *p. 2*; 23, *p. 57*)	Aleut of Nikolski (10, *p. 506*)
		Eskimo of Mackenzie Delta (69, *p. 225*)
Subarctic		Kaska (68, *p. 590*)
Northwest Coast		Northwest Coast Indians (107, *pp. 310, 362, 363*) 3 Salish tribes (108, *p. 92*)
Plateau	Klamath (38, *p. 18*)	
Plains		Oglala Sioux (129, *p. 43*)
Prairies	Dakota Sioux (74, *p. 229*) Standing Rock Sioux (212, *p. 476*)	Indians of Omaha (103, *p. 536*) Potawotami of "Whitehorse" (58, *p. 289*)
Desert	Uintah-Ouray No. Ute (239, *p. 20*)	
Oasis	Hopi (102, *p. 717*; 112, *p. 117*; 113, *p. 233*)	Mescalero Apache (27, *p. 120*); Navaho (47, *p. 163*); (63, *pp. 123, 129*); (169, *p. 11*)
Indians of North America	High-school students (13, *p. 25*)	"American Indians" (36, *p. 72*) Certain Canadian reserves, only? (28, *pp. 22, 25*)
Miscellaneous		Indians of Chicago, various tribes (116, *p. 71*; 117, *p. 1778*)
Unknown		Anonymous Indian communities (97, *p. 3*); (152, *p. 4*)

ᵃ Citations joined by braces constitute single accounts. See footnote 15, Chapter 4.

areas at all, it would seem most likely to show up in the case of a symptom which has been rated CONFLICTING EVIDENCE. To investigate this possibility, the distribution of one of these, i.e., solitary drinking (Symptom 16A), is presented in Chart 2. In the culture areas where evidence is available for more than one tribe, i.e., Arctic Coast, Prairies, Oasis, the symptom is rated PRESENT in some groups and ABSENT—RARE in others. Of course, the homogeneity which obtains in the Driver and Massey (37) culture area groups used here is only relative. Customs and values do vary within these, and perhaps that is what the distribution reflects. A great deal more evidence would be necessary, however, to demonstrate this with any certainty.

The distribution of the occurrence of solitary drinking does not seem to correspond to community type; at least, all-Indian communities have been rated in both categories. However, the two urban groups represented (Omaha and Chicago) are both rated ABSENT–RARE. Size of group is not obviously implicated in the distribution; small and large groups appear in both columns.

The presentation of data thus far has been oriented toward the symptoms, documenting the groups in which each does or does not occur according to the literature. This does not, however, give a picture of the occurrence of constellations of symptoms in individual groups. To partly counteract this distortion, I present in Table 6 a summary of ratings of symptoms in the Standing Rock Sioux, chosen because Whittaker's work (212, 213), on which it is based, provides some evidence on more of the behaviors contained in Jellinek's list than most studies.

Most of the symptoms rated PRESENT are reported by a proportion of Standing Rock Sioux higher than the estimated proportion of

TABLE 6.—*Ratings of Occurrence of 12 Symptoms of Alcohol Addiction among Standing Rock Sioux Drinkers**

Symptom	PRESENT	ABSENT	Reference
1. Alcoholic palimpsests	42% "had experienced"		212, p. 475
5. Guilt feelings about drinking		x	213, p. 86
7. Increasing frequency of palimpsests	25% of those who "had experienced them"		212, p. 475
8. "Loss of control"	37%		212, p. 476
Inability to abstain	45%		212, p. 475
10. Social pressures (countered)		x	213, p. 86
12. Marked aggressive behavior	x		213, p. 83
15. Changing the pattern of drinking	76%		212, p. 476
16A. Solitary drinking	10%		212, p. 476
27. Hospitalization: alcoholic cirrhosis	14%		212, p. 476
30. Regular morning drinking	9% "regularly," 16% "occasionally"		212, p. 475
31. Prolonged intoxications	over 50%		212, p. 476
34. Alcoholic psychoses	9% (delirium tremens)		212, p. 476

* Based on Whittaker (212, 213).

alcohol addicts in the general population—about 4% according to a government report (199, *p. 10*). A better gauge would be a comparison of rates of the individual symptoms in Indians with rates in drinkers in the general population. Rates for three of these symptoms were obtained by Mulford and Wilson (149, *p. 19*) in a population of Cedar Rapids residents, including separate rates in "drinkers" and "known [active] alcoholics." Unfortunately, however, these investigators did not report rates of the individual symptoms; instead they grouped sets of three symptoms together and reported the percentage of respondents who acknowledged experiencing two of the three. However, using these rates as though they applied to each of the three items in the sets, we can make comparisons with Whittaker's data, shown in Table 6.

Symptom 4, avid drinking, reported in 42% of the standing Rock Sioux drinkers, was found in 4% of Cedar Rapids drinkers and 14% of known alcoholics there; Symptom 30, morning drinking, 9% regularly and 16% occasionally in the Sioux, 1% and 10% in Cedar Rapids drinkers and alcoholics; and Symptom 31, prolonged intoxications, over 50% in the Sioux, 1% and 21% in the Cedar Rapids drinkers and alcoholics. It thus appears that the Standing Rock Sioux report these three symptoms at far higher rates than "drinkers," and even than the "known [active] alcoholics" in Cedar Rapids. Nevertheless, before we could draw firm conclusions from this comparison, we would need rates for more symptoms, and the problem of weighting symptoms would remain.

From the discussion so far, it should be clear that I do not believe the tally of ratings of symptoms, weighted or not, either supports or refutes the nonaddiction hypothesis decisively. There seems to be general agreement that a few symptoms of alcohol addiction as defined by Jellinek do not occur in many of the groups covered; a few others do occur. But for most of the symptoms we have either conflicting evidence or insufficient evidence to justify rating their occurrence (much less incidence) among the Indian groups covered in the literature. More important, even if we had better data, it is not at all clear that the symptoms interpreted in the dominant society as indicators of alcohol addiction should be so interpreted when they occur among Indians.

6

Summary Tally of Opinions

THE PRECEDING TEST of the reverse-firewater hypothesis was indecisive. The available evidence on the occurrence of the Jellinek symptoms, whether alone or in combination, has failed either to prove or disprove the proposition that alcohol addiction is rare among North American Indians. However, the question can be explored a bit further through a weaker alternative test of the reverse-firewater hypothesis. This test consists of a tally of the opinions expressed in "accounts" which address the question of whether or not alcohol addiction occurs in the groups they observed, regardless of the criteria (usually unstated) on which these opinions are based.

Not all of the statements cited in this opinion tally employ the term "alcohol addiction." This presents problems of interpretation, as discussed in Chapter 3. When the term "alcoholism" or "alcoholic" has been used, I have followed Keller and Seeley's rule (96, *p. 19, footnote 7*) that unless the two are distinguished, "the term alcoholism must be understood as probably including alcohol addiction." I take the term "chronic alcoholic" to be equivalent to "alcohol addict," as well. Jellinek once tried to distinguish the two, but "this distinction did not prevail" (96, *p. 9*).

In tallying opinions, I have used the same system employed in tallying "accounts" of the occurrence of symptoms. That is, statements by joint authors constitute a single opinion, as do multiple statements by the same author, even if he generalizes at two different levels,[1] or if he expresses the same opinion about one or more separate groups of Indians. The theoretically possible (or even probable) case of one author claiming that addiction is present in one group and not in another has not occurred. In cases where I have relied on secondary sources, I count the author of the opinion quoted, not the author of the work in which it appears, unless the latter expresses an independent opinion.

---

[1]E.g., Lemert in one work (108) covers three Salish tribes and in another (107) "Northwest Coast Indians."

I emphasize that the opinions I attribute to an author are my own interpretation of his statements and the context in which they occur in the literature on Indian drinking. I hope the ratings coincide with the author's conception of his stand on the reverse-firewater hypothesis. It should be remembered that most of these statements were casual observations which the authors could not have anticipated would be used for the present purpose. For this reason, I originally had hoped to confirm ratings with the authors before publication. This proved impractical for more than a few, since the ratings had to be considered in the context of the entire manuscript. Few of the authors with whom I did check the rating assigned to their opinion on the occurrence of alcohol addiction among American Indians were willing to endorse its categorization into one of three arbitrary pigeonholes, i.e., PRESENT, ABSENT–RARE, or UNDECIDED. Therefore, some strenuous objections seem inevitable.

In the literature on Indian drinking covered herein, 33 authors address the question of whether or not alcohol addiction occurs in the group they report on. For the preceding test (Chapter 5), nearly 100 "accounts" were cited in support of the symptom ratings. However, none of these provided evidence on a large number of

CHART 3.—*Summary Tally of Opinions on Occurrence of Alcohol Addiction*

	ABSENT-RARE	PRESENT	UNDECIDED
Arctic Coast			
Aleut of Nikolski	Berreman (10)		
Eskimo and Indians of Kaktovik	Chance (21)		
Subarctic			
Kaska	Honigmanns (68)		
Northwest Coast			
3 Salish tribes	Lemert (107, 108)		
Kwakiutl	Rohners (165)		
Plateau			
Klamath		Du Toit (38)	
Plains			
Kiowa-Apache	Freeman (52)		
Oglala Sioux		Mindell (237)	

[cont.]

CHART 3.—cont.

	ABSENT-RARE	PRESENT	UNDECIDED
Prairies			
Standing Rock Sioux		Whittaker (212)	
Potawatomi of "Whitehorse"	Hamer (58, 59)		
Indians of Omaha		Kuttner & Lorincz (103)	
Desert			
Duck Valley Reservation			Manning (125)
Uintah-Ouray Northern Ute			Slater (238, 239)
Oasis			
"Indians"	McKinley (123)		
Mescalero Apache		Boyer (14)	
Mohave	Devereux (33)		
Navaho	Heath (62, 63) Szuter et al. (187) Wellman[a] Werner[a] (and 209)	Ferguson (47, 48) Henderson (65) Savard (169)	
Indians of North America	Dozier (36) Sanchez (168) Wagner[b] Dailey (28, 29)		
Miscellaneous (several culture areas combined)	Littman (117)	Baker (5) Hawthorn (61)	Brody (16)
Unknown (*Anonymous Community*)	B.I.A. official[c]	Krutz[d]	
Totals	19	11	3

[a] Quoted by McKinley (123).
[b] Quoted by Fahy and Muschenheim (40).
[c] Quoted by Officer (152).
[d] Quoted by Keneally (97).

symptoms. Therefore, the sample of 33 for the opinion test actually is considerably larger than was available for most of the single items in the symptom test.

As shown in Chart 3, among the 33 opinions which have been assigned a rating, I interpret 19 as advocating the reverse-firewater hypothesis that alcohol addiction is ABSENT or RARE in the Indian groups to which they refer. These statements already have been quoted.[2] They refer to a variety of groups in a number of diverse culture areas.

These opinions are expressed by 12 anthropologists, 5 physicians, 2 Bureau of Indian Affairs staff members, 2 social workers, 1 educator, and 1 alcoholism treatment program executive.[3] A majority of the opinions in support of the reverse-firewater hypothesis refer to Indians who live on reservations or in other predominantly Indian communities, but urban Indians of various tribal origins also are included.

I interpret the statements of 11 authors as reporting that alcohol addiction is PRESENT in the groups in question. I count these as opponents of the reverse-firewater hypothesis. The statements so interpreted are quoted or paraphrased in the following paragraphs.

Speaking of 36 federal prison inmates of various tribal origins (half were Sioux or Apache), Baker (5, *p. 274*) says, "Most of the 36 could be correctly labeled as chronic alcoholic in their tendencies."

Boyer (14, *p. 236*) says he treated and cured cases of "chronic alcoholism" during 12 months of field work among the Mescalero Apache.

Du Toit (38, *p. 19*) describes a group of "lone wolves" among the Klamath who are looked down upon by the rest of the population because their drinking has "the regularity to classify them as alcoholics."

Ferguson (48, *p. 902*) says the Navaho patients in the Gallup treatment program "could well fulfill the World Health Organization definition of alcoholism." Elsewhere (47, *p. 167*) she refers specifically to addictive drinking: "What is distinctive about Navaho drinking is the presence of forces which promote addictive recreation drinking without adequate counter forces to control it."

Hawthorn et al. (61, *p. 12*) say:

"By now some Indians are habitual drinkers. This raises the question as to whether some of the Indians who drink excessively are properly classified as alcoholics. Very few Indians have been officially recognized as such, but little special attention has been paid to the possibility. We believe that officials tend to disregard the presence of alcoholism among Indians, and that as a result some Indians who may be regarded as alcoholics do not get help and treatment they need."

[2]Chapter 1, pp. 5–8.

[3]The number of professions exceeds the number of "opinions" because it seemed appropriate in the first case to count each joint author separately and in the second to count them as one.

Henderson (65, *p. 68*) reports:

"Not all members of our research treatment staff [Community Treatment Plan for Navajo Problem Drinkers] were convinced prior to commencing work on the problem that any Navajos were really alcoholic,' nor were they convinced that the Navajo rates of drinking and arrest were indicative of Navajo drinking problems. Some staff members had to see the arrest records of the Gallup Police Department and read a report by Stewart on Indian arrests and other cross-cultural studies on alcoholism before they were convinced that Indian drunkenness was not just an historical stereotype. Furthermore, exploring of the literature emphasizes the widespread nature of Indian alcoholism."

Keneally (97, *p. 3*) describes three types of problem drinkers identified by Gordon Krutz (then a U. S. Public Health Service educator) in an anonymous Indian community: *(a)* the prealcoholic, mainly confined to youths; *(b)* the plain alcoholic—the "weekender" who is able to drink and hold a job, but has conflict with the family; *(c)* the "chronic" alcoholic, who has lost all hope for the present and future, cannot hold a job, and is in conflict with his family and society.

Kuttner and Lorincz (103) appear to restrict the term "addiction" to drug use, which also is discussed in their article. However, I interpret their statements about the occurrence of "alcoholism" in the group concerned (e.g., *pp. 530, 531, 536, 539*) as referring to addictive drinking.

Mindell (237, *p. 8*) discusses a number of obstacles to treating problem drinkers among the Oglala Sioux. Among these, he includes "myth." "One of these is that there are no alcoholics amongst Indians, only a lot of drinkers—this is not so."

Concerning 200 Navaho disulfiram-therapy patients at Fort Defiance Indian Hospital, Savard (169, *p. 911, footnote 4*) says: "All alcoholics treated not only were alcoholics by self-admission but met the World Health Organization criteria for alcoholism. Nonalcoholics met none of the W.H.O. criteria." Interpretation of this statement is somewhat complicated by the fact that Savard does not say which W.H.O. definition he means. The "alcoholics" of the 1951 version became the "excessive drinkers" of the 1952 version. Furthermore, in the 1952 version, both addictive and nonaddictive drinkers are subsumed under the label "alcoholics." I am assuming, perhaps incorrectly, that Savard refers to the 1952 version and Jellinek's criteria. If this interpretation is correct, the statement quoted above seems to represent a shift by Savard from his earlier view as a participant in Szuter et al. (187, *p. 1*) advocating the reverse-firewater hypothesis.

Whittaker (212, *p. 475*) describes the occurrence of a number of Jellinek's symptoms of alcohol addiction among the Standing Rock Sioux and comments: "Some of the signs mentioned may, of course, not be related to alcoholism in this particular culture. Others, such as delirium tremens, are undoubtedly indicative of alcoholism."

Chart 3 (under PRESENT) summarizes the groups referred to by these 11 opponents of the reverse-firewater hypothesis and their culture area distribution. Comparison with the ABSENT–RARE column reveals that division of opinion about the occurrence of alcohol addiction among Indians is not characterized by complementary distribution among different Indian groups. That is, the Navaho appear in both columns. The proportion of nonurban to urban groups represented is about the same in both columns.

"Opponents" of the reverse-firewater hypothesis include three physicians, five anthropologists, two psychologists, one biochemist, one social worker, one psychiatrist, and one Public Health Service educator. When we compare the fields of specialization of these "opponents" with those of the "proponents" cited earlier, it seems clear that differing viewpoints among professions do not account for the division of opinion as to whether or not alcohol addiction occurs among Indians. Disagreements within professions are more marked than those among professions. Alcohol addictions is considered PRESENT by some and ABSENT–RARE by other representatives of the same profession.

The balance of the works which discuss the possible occurrence of alcohol addiction in the groups they cover have been rated UN-DECIDED.

The first example documents how confusing the concept of "alcoholism" can be to Indians. Manning (125), a social worker and member of the Paiute-Shoshone Tribes of the Duck Valley Reservation (Nevada and Idaho), reports a discussion which occurred in a meeting to consider the advisability of establishing an alcoholism program on the reservation. The following questions were asked (125, *p. 2*): "Who is an alcoholic? (Is he a sick man? A bad man? Are all Indians who drink alcoholics, or just the winos?) Is the Indian drinker an alcoholic? Is he a social drinker? Is he a periodic drinker?" These questions, and the context in which they occurred, suggest that members of this meeting of Indians, including the author, were trying to figure out for themselves what the dominant society means by an "alcohol addict" and other alcohol-associated labels, and whether or not these are applicable within their group.

On the other hand, one of the members, commenting on a meeting with visiting, non-Indian Alcoholics Anonymous members, seemed all too willing to swallow the dominant-society concepts whole:

"One of these men helped to clarify a question I had and that was, who is an alcoholic? I learned that an alcoholic can be a person who drinks every day, every two months, or more, as long as his drinking creates a problem, and he has lost control of his drinking."

Manning's description (125, *pp. 6, 7*) of the Indians' reaction to the behavior of the visiting A.A.s is extremely interesting:

"At the end of the meeting there was a spell of silence. The Indians' reaction seemed that of withdrawal and embarrassment."

After the visitors left, comments by Indians included the following (125, *pp. 6, 7*):

"I thought I had big problems, but they are small compared to some of their problems."

"It was a surprise to me that White people couldn't control themselves any better than us Indians."

"I don't think most Indians will discuss in public their personal problems, especially drinking experiences."

"I didn't understand how a person refuses a drink from their best friends."

Despite some of the negative comments, Manning (125, *p. 7*) reports that the tribal members liked the sincerity, honesty and the humbleness of the people who spoke. The Tribe decided to organize an alcoholism program. Although it included group meetings, the Indians worked out their own procedures, which were quite different from the Alcoholics Anonymous format.[4]

Slater (238, *p. 1*) seems to lean toward the proposition that alcohol addiction is rare among Indians of the Uintah-Ouray, but really sidesteps the issue:

"While excessive drinking was easily recognized, there were wide differences of opinion concerning whether we were looking at widespread

[4]Manning, L. Personal communication, 1973.

alcoholism or whether the drinking was still largely under individual control. . . .

"I do not plan to use this term [alcoholic] in referring to those included in this study, however. I have never fully accepted its use in describing the Indian problem drinker because there are so many aspects of their drinking that are different from that of the non-Indian alcoholic. I prefer to think of them simply as problem drinkers or excessive drinkers."

Brody (16, *p. 8*) says that among Indian residents of a Canadian urban Skid Row "many of the older men and women are alcohol-dependent." The latter term is frequently used as a synonym for addiction. However, in another passage (*p. 73*), he seems to say the opposite: "It is essential to realize that where alcohol is a real pleasure, and heavy consumption is regular [as he says it is in the group he covers], the kinds of explanations which might cover non-Indian norms of drinking—the occasional fling or pathological alcoholism—are unlikely to apply." If he intends "pathological alcoholism" to be synonymous with alcohol addiction, and if, by equating this with non-Indian drinking, he means to imply it does not occur in his group, the statement should be rated ABSENT–RARE. In Brody's case, the rating UNDECIDED means that I am not sure what he means, rather than that he has not formed an opinion.

Despite the small number of statements classified as UNDECIDED about the reverse-firewater hypothesis, there still is some distribution among areas, and both urban and nonurban groups are represented, as shown in Chart 3. The professions involved are a social worker (Indian), a personnel and guidance specialist, and an anthropologist.

As summarized in Chart 3, among the 33 observers who address the question of the possible occurrence of alcohol addiction in various Indian groups, 19 (58%) express opinions which I interpret to mean that they consider alcohol addiction ABSENT or RARE. Of the remaining 14, 11 seem to think alcohol addiction is PRESENT in their particular group. I have rated 3 as UNDECIDED.

Once again, due to the varying levels of generalization employed by the authors, numbers alone would not be decisive even if they were not so evenly divided.

Comparison of culture areas is not very revealing, either. Addiction is rated ABSENT–RARE in all the groups represented in three culture areas (Arctic Coast, Subarctic, Northwest Coast). In the Plateau area, represented by only one group, it is rated PRESENT. In the remaining three areas (Plains, Prairies, Oasis), as well as in my categories "miscellaneous" and "unknown," both PRESENT and ABSENT–RARE ratings occur. Although it is quite possible that significant differences in the incidence of "alcohol addiction" could be manifested among culture areas, the distribution of the ratings seems equivocal, and may simply reflect accident of observation or differences in definition of the term.

The distribution of ratings within culture areas is not clear-cut, either. Levy and Kunitz (112, 113) have suggested the possibility of significant alcohol-related differences among groups in the same culture area. Thus, the differences in group ratings might reflect actual differences in the incidence of alcohol addiction. However, given the dearth of hard data on which most of the opinions are based, differences in conceptions of alcohol addiction seem to provide a more likely explanation than actual intra-area differences.

The same holds true of contradictory ratings for the same group. The Navaho appear in both the ABSENT–RARE and PRESENT columns. This might reflect actual differences in incidence among the samples of the same population the disagreeing authors have observed. However, the only data so far available which seem sufficiently detailed and conceptually sound to support inter- and intragroup comparisons are those of Levy and Kunitz.

Since the concept "alcohol addiction" represents a higher order of abstraction than the individual symptoms thereof, the ratings of opinion are even more subject to errors of interpretation than those on individual symptoms. And since few authors clearly define their particular category "alcohol addiction," we may be adding together things the authors would consider to be quite different phenomena. I hope I have not misrepresented opinions, or attributed any to an author who actually is undecided. The statements quoted herein have been used to illustrate general pitfalls in trying to evaluate the occurrence of alcohol addiction in any group, and particularly in Indian groups. I trust the authors will agree that such pitfalls exist, and that the urgent need to pinpoint them justifies the use I have made of their data.

Levy and Kunitz are conspicuously absent from the foregoing summary tally of opinion. Although they have provided clear evidence, cited earlier, of high rates of occurrence of some manifestations interpreted as symptoms of alcohol addiction in the dominant society, they have so far published only brief and guarded comments about the occurrence of alcohol addiction in the Southwest Indian groups whose drinking they have studied in relatively great detail.

Few observers would seem as well qualified to assess the validity of the nonaddiction myth, so their restraint should give us pause. The caution they exhibit seems to stem in part from their data indicating wide variation in alcohol-related characteristics among and even within Indian groups. (These findings emphasize the vulnerability of generalizations about "Indian" drinking, and suggest that the literature may have overemphasized similarities in alcohol-related characteristics among Indian groups.) But more important, these authors suspect that cultural influences, such as style of drinking, traditional values, and social organization, may influence the incidence of manifestations interpreted by the dominant society as symptomatic of alcohol addiction to such a degree that the significance of their occurrence among Indians should be interpreted with great care.

Out of context, two recent statements by these authors seem to show signs of leaning toward the idea that the phenomenon labeled alcohol addiction by the dominant society is rare among the Indians they have observed. They say:

"It is clear that Indian drinking differs appreciably from drinking in our own society. Despite the fact that there is considerable evidence to suggest that severe problems, both physiological and social, exist in Indian societies, it is not clear that the disease we call alcoholism is the same in both White and Indian societies or even that there is one unified pathology we can call alcoholism" (113, *p. 234*).

"The question that needs to be asked is whether this behavior [i.e., what is considered diagnostic of deviant drinking by White society] truly represents alcoholism as we are used to diagnosing it in White chronic alcoholics. Our findings lead us to answer negatively" (113, *p. 230*).

Taken as a whole, however, Levy and Kunitz's work to date seems to indicate that in a cross-cultural situation they have not yet discovered a satisfactory way to detect or measure phenomena which would be appropriately labeled addiction. Thus, these authors, who are among the most experienced and esteemed students of alcohol use by Indians, are not yet ready to express an opinion as to whether or not alcohol addiction occurs among the Indians they have observed.

The opinions of Levy and Kunitz might have been rated UNDECIDED. However, since I have explored the question at some depth with them but not with the other authors, to be fair I have excluded them from the summary tally of opinion.

7

Conclusions

CASUAL INSPECTION of literature on drinking in a number of
North American Indian groups leaves a strong first impression
that something called "alcohol addiction" is rare among them. Closer
scrutiny reveals disagreement on the subject. Neither a tally of evidence on the occurrence of individual symptoms nor a summation of
opinion on the occurrence of "alcohol addiction," regardless of the
criteria used, clearly supports or discredits the reverse-firewater hypothesis that alcohol addiction is rare among Indians.

In the sense that it is undocumented, the reverse-firewater hypothesis seems to be a myth. Furthermore, until the hypothesis is
tested against adequate data in a suitable theoretical framework,
the possibility remains open that it may merit another connotation
of the term "myth," i.e., false.

Truth or falsity, however, is not the only issue. Myths are powerful influences in human affairs: they condition situations, their preconceptions create consequences. Before the reverse-firewater myth
receives any further endorsement in the literature, it requires a
great deal more scrutiny.

Disagreement as to whether or not alcohol addiction occurs among
Indians seems to result from both factual and theoretical controversy.

First, the disagreement reflects conflicting evidence on the occurrence of specific manifestations. In some cases these factual disputes
may reflect actual differences among and within Indian groups of
the incidence of alleged symptoms of alcohol addiction; this may,
in turn, result from differences in drinking styles or other variables.
In some other cases the variation in findings may merely reflect difficulties of data gathering, as described herein and by Levy and Kunitz
(113, *pp. 218–220*).

More often, however, the disagreements appear to result from
theoretical confusion about what should be observed, i.e., from the
absence of standardized criteria for "alcohol addiction," and how
observations should be interpreted.

If all observers would investigate the rate of incidence of a standard set of symptoms in the groups they report upon, at least the variable of differential indicators would be eliminated. Jellinek's list, for example, suggests many topics for observation and analysis which students of Indian drinking have not yet reported upon. The use of such an instrument, whether Jellinek's or some other, probably would improve the quantity and quality of evidence about North American Indian drinking. The resulting data might make possible a more adequate test of the reverse-firewater hypothesis than is possible with the information we now have. As the foregoing discussion has suggested, however, so far we do not have a checklist of symptoms which would be adequate for investigating the incidence of alcohol addiction even in the dominant society, much less in subgroups such as Indians, or in other cultures. Furthermore, in addition to the practical problems involved, MacAndrew[1] points out theoretical grounds for suggesting that the establishment of definitive sets of "recognition rules" may be "*in principle* impossible of accomplishment," even in the apparently simpler case of "drunkenness."

Confusion about what constitute valid indicators of alcohol addiction will continue pending clarification of the concept. Empirical discoveries may one day solve the problem. In the meantime, as long as the diagnostic category "alcohol addict" continues to be used and must be based on manifestations which are at least partly culturally determined and defined, we should at least try to delineate these criteria more precisely. As a minimum, people who discuss alcohol addiction should say what they mean by the term. The very process of developing explicit criteria for one's folk category "alcohol addict" sharpens awareness of the problems with the concept and discourages unwarranted generalizations on the subject.

Dissatisfaction with the concept of alcohol addiction is reflected in discussions about the propriety of considering it as a disease.[2] These arguments, however, tend to divert attention from what seems to me to be a more important question: What is alcohol addiction? More precisely, to what construct, if any, may this label be appropriately applied?

The term "alcohol addict" seems to connote qualitative differences

---

[1]In an important statement which appeared too late to be discussed here or included in the bibliography; i.e., "On the notion of drunkenness," In: PATTISON, E. M. et al., eds., Emerging concepts of alcohol dependence. [In press.]

[2]See, e.g., Jellinek (84); MacAndrew (120); and Robinson (164).

between the people so labeled and other drinkers. We might decide that we should reserve the term in case qualitative differences are one day discovered. It seems possible, however, that the differences are merely quantitative. Even so, the label could appropriately be used to describe a set of quantitative differences which set "alcohol addicts" apart from other drinkers, provided we could agree upon clear, though arbitrarily defined, measurable limits for a range of physiological and behavioral manifestations at the end of a continuum of drinking that the label could appropriately represent. So far such limits have not been adequately defined for any group.

Pending either the discovery of qualitative differences or standardization of a set of suitable quantitative differences to distinguish alcohol addicts from other drinkers, perhaps we should consider abandoning the label. Indeed, Eddy et al. (39, *p. 726*), on behalf of the World Health Organization, have suggested substituting the term "alcohol dependence" for "alcohol addiction." Unfortunately, however, the new label seems to cover the same vague construct as the old, and to elude definition as persistently. Other authorities are also questioning the utility of the construct "alcohol addiction" with increasing frequency. For example, Cahalan (17, *p. 4*) rejected the concept "alcohol addiction" in general, and Jellinek's version in particular, because it "has been seized upon by many in the medical profession (and others who are physiologically oriented) to maintain a wide conceptual gap between the alcoholic and the allegedly nonaddictive problem drinker—a gap which a growing number of public health workers believe is detrimental to a better understanding and control of problem drinking." Thus the concept "alcohol addict" may be not only useless, but perhaps even harmful, because it implies vast and easily detectable differences, whether qualitative or quantitative, between those so labeled and other categories of drinkers. The existence and nature of such differences remain open questions pending further research. In the meantime, use of the term "alcohol addict" may influence people to prejudge the answers.

Diagnostic categories, King (98, *p. 332*) points out, "are not given in experience as such but they are created out of experience." Therefore, when experience has demonstrated that one of these, such as "alcohol addict," is not only useless but harmful, presumably it should be discarded.

On the other hand, arguments in favor of retaining the concept "alcohol addict" might be based on evidence of similarities between people so labeled and those labeled "opiate addicts." Recent studies underscore the resemblance between symptoms of withdrawal from the two drugs. For example, Davis and Walsh (31, *p. 1005*) say, "It seems possible that the addictions may be similar and that the real distinctions between the two drugs could be only length of time and dosage required for the development of dependence." In other words, there may be purely quantitative differences between "opiate addicts" and alcohol users who exhibit withdrawal symptoms. If so, it would seem appropriate, by analogy, to refer to these alcohol users as "addicts." This would follow, of course, only if we agree that the label "addict" is appropriate for opiate users who show signs of physical dependence when the drug is withdrawn. A discussion of this topic is beyond the scope of this study. However, the World Health Organization (39, *p. 722*) has recommended abandoning the term "addiction" for opiates as well as for alcohol. This action suggests that in practice the concept "addiction" has proved no more useful for opiates than for alcohol.

Many observers of Indian drinking apparently are unaware that "alcohol addiction" is not a well-defined phenomenon and that there is little agreement as to what manifestations constitute valid indicators of the diagnostic category. The alcohol literature is very large and scattered. Most people who have not consulted this literature hold the "commonsense" conviction that everybody knows an "alcohol addict" when he sees one.

It is possible to disabuse oneself of this conviction with a minimum of effort by consulting definitions of "alcohol addiction," "alcoholism," and the terms used in these definitions, provided in a compendium by Keller and McCormick (95). If this exercise were mandatory for anyone publishing on the subject of drinking, it would go a long way toward eliminating the basis for Washburne's general criticism (208, *p. 12*) of cross-cultural studies of alcohol use: "Work on the use of alcohol in various societies has not advanced significantly because it has not been cumulative. Each researcher has tended to make the same mistakes, leave the same omissions, as he starts at the same naive level of his predecessors."

On the other hand, to their credit, I suspect that observers of Indian drinking who refuse to label Indians as "alcohol addicts" are reluctant to do so, not only because of their recognition of differences between Indian and White drinking characteristics, but also because of their largely intuitive recognition that the concept of addiction is unduly vague and arbitrary. If these observers were to scrutinize drinking in the dominant society as carefully as they have in Indian groups they might find themselves as reluctant to use the label "alcohol addict" in the former as in the latter.

Anthropologists have skills which, if combined with some knowledge of the alcohol literature, could make welcome contributions to investigations of the concept "alcohol addiction." Studies of stereotyping and of cultural constructs are specialties of the discipline. Sorting out the culture-bound from the culture-free requires the cross-cultural perspective which anthropologists are best qualified to supply. Furthermore, the ethnoscience methods developed by anthropologists seem well suited to a new approach to studies of drinking behavior. These methods attempt to overcome a difficulty described by MacAndrew (120, p. 499):

"All facts are necessarily and from the outset preinterpreted facts, rooted in what Whitehead once termed 'the whole apparatus of common sense thought.'
"What guarantee have we that the products of our inquiries will be immune to whatsoever consequence might derive from the fact that, in simple truth, we are no less 'of the world' and are thus no less subject to the force of our fundamental insight than are those whom we study?"

Total reliance on "common sense" is perhaps even more hazardous in studying other cultures than in investigating our own. In either, preconceptions can lead to finding what was expected, whether it is there or not.

Ethnoscience approaches are designed to minimize such bias by discovering how phenomena are organized and communicated in a particular group, and describing the pertinent behavior in terms of these categories, rather than in terms of the investigator's a priori categories, in order to increase the objectivity of description, analysis and interpretation and thus the cultural relevance of the data.

By analogy with linguistic terminology, the ethnoscience approach has been described as "emic." The use of a priori categories is sometimes described by the contrasting term "etic," but this usage is not entirely accurate. Etic categories may be a priori categories, but they also may be constructed from common categories discovered through comparative emic studies.[3] Ethnoscience methodologists do not object to the latter practice; in fact that is their goal.

---

[3]Goodenough (55, pp. 113–114, footnote 15) makes a convincing argument for this sequence of study, and his last chapter provides a recent, succinct explanation of these two approaches to description.

To the degree that Jellinek incorporated some of the diagnostic signs suggested by Alcoholics Anonymous members into his list of symptoms of "alcohol addiction," he made a step in the direction of ethnoscience methodology. Wilkins and Wesson (214, *p. 74*), a psychologist and a sociologist, suggested an intensification of this approach. They said:

"A further need is the development of better ways of diagnosing and identifying alcoholics. One suggestion is to study the ways in which alcoholics identify themselves. What clues do A.A. members use when they say 'He's one of us'? It may well be profitable to spell out these clues, and any others which are present. They should help us find groups in the population which have a high yield of alcoholism."

Spradley (182) has used an ethnoscience approach in investigating a number of aspects of the lives of urban nomads and has obtained some pertinent data on categories of drinkers as incidental parts of his other componential definitions.[4] MacAndrew's (120, *p. 499*) suggested empirical study to discover the diagnostic clues by which physicians label people "alcohol addict" is in the spirit of ethnoscience, except that he proposes to begin with what may be an a priori category, "alcohol addiction," rather than by discovering what "emic" categories of drinkers exist.

Thus, several specialists have suggested the application of ethnoscience methods to alcohol research, but so far no published accounts of such studies have appeared.[5] If this emic approach were used in studying the drinking behavior of many groups in this and in other countries, we might find that each culture, and perhaps even each subculture, uses a unique set of categories and diagnostic signs. If so, this would indicate that the concepts are entirely culturally rel-

[4]Spradley, J. P. Personal communication, 10 August 1970.

[5]An insider's view is used to varying degrees in work concerning Indian drinking in progress by anthropologists Michael W. Everett (University of Kentucky, on White Mountain Apache), Martin D. Topper (University of Chicago, on Navaho), Jack O. Waddell ("Drink, friend!" Social contexts of convivial drinking and drunkenness among Papago Indians in an urban setting. Proc. 1st Annu. Alcsm Conf. NIAAA, pp. 237-251, 1973). I have conducted studies aimed at discovering the folk drinking style categories recognized by residents of an Indian settlement. The National Institute on Alcohol Abuse and Alcoholism has supported a pilot project called "Indian Alcohol Users: An Insider's View" (Grant No. R-18-MH-22524) and a study titled "Handling Liquor in a Nevada Indian Community" (Grant No. 1-RO1-AA01352-01). My Ph.D. dissertation (University of California, Irvine, 1975) is a numerical folk taxonomy of Indian drinking styles.

ative and that cross-cultural comparison would be difficult and perhaps impossible.

On the other hand, ethnoscience studies might reveal common elements in the taxonomies of drinkers in all these cultures and subcultures which then would constitute a set of cross-culturally valid etic categories of drinkers and diagnostic markers thereof. This taxonomy might or might not include a category corresponding to a construct which could appropriately be labeled "alcohol addict."

Among medical practitioners in this country it seems fairly certain we would find an emic category labeled "alcohol addict." MacAndrew (120, *p. 499*) has suggested that this group would provide the ideal target population for initial studies of how drinkers are classified in the category "alcohol addict." Indeed, if we are to begin with the preconceived category "alcohol addict," it would be best to investigate it in a group where we can be fairly certain the category is emic, i.e., in the subculture which created the category. MacAndrew (120, *p. 499*) says:

"I know of no empirical study addressed specifically to the actual procedures used by medical practitioners in determining the warranted applicability of the designation 'alcoholic' to a series of individual cases. And neither, apparently, does the Surgeon General of the United States Public Health Service, who, after consulting with the staff of the National Office of Vital Statistics . . . was informed that 'while the Standard Nomenclature of Diseases does list the various types of alcoholic conditions, definitions are not given and it is not possible to know the criteria used by physicians in completing death certificates.' [Nevertheless] the condition entered on the death certificate is accepted as final by the National Office of Vital Statistics. . . . The lack of precision . . . arises from the fact that there is no generally accepted clear-cut definition of what constitutes chronic alcoholism."

In the case of living patients, practitioners' criteria for the diagnostic category "alcoholic" seem to be equally mysterious. Thus, determination of how physicians identify the people they classify as "alcoholics" or "alcohol addicts" would seem to be long overdue. MacAndrew says (120, *p. 499*), "Such an investigation would clearly seem to be the next step. Indeed, logically, it would seem to be the first step." An ethnoscience approach might well be appropriate for the suggested inquiry since, despite their status as authoritative diagnosticians, the medical practitioners' category "alcoholic" or "alcohol addict" may turn out to have more basis in folk wisdom than in science.

A study of how American medical practitioners arrive at the label "alcohol addict" might reveal that, despite the confusion in definitions and theoretical assumptions, members of this group share a common set of diagnostic criteria for the category "alcohol addict." Many people, presumably including the U.S. Surgeon General and the National Office of Vital Statistics, would like to know what these criteria are. Even if the studies only revealed the extent of disagreement in the criteria used by the group, this too would be an improvement over the present state of affairs. If students of alcohol use who created the category "alcohol addict" have produced a vast literature on the subject without being able to specify what an "alcohol addict" is or how one can be identified, ethnoscience studies could make a useful contribution by documenting and dramatizing this fact. Such findings might, for example, convince physicians that the category "alcohol addict" is useless and should be abandoned. The fact that "alcohol addict" probably is an emic category among American medical practitioners doesn't make it inviolable. Ethnoscientists do not claim the folk categories they discover and describe are any more "real" than the a priori categories they decry. But they do claim that these categories, because they are a part of the conceptual world of the group that uses them, can influence, and indeed are a part of, that group's behavior. If this behavior is to be understood, the criteria for the categories must be made explicit.

Whether the findings were positive (a standardized set of diagnostic signs) or negative (documentation of the lack of standardized criteria), ethnoscience studies of the medical practitioners' construct "alcohol addict" could eliminate a lot of confusion. However, ethnoscience methods probably are not yet sufficiently developed for adaptation to the complications introduced by the scientism of the target population "medical practitioners."

As an alternative, "drinkers" might provide a population more suitable for ethnoscience techniques. Assuming that "drinkers" constitutes an emic category in the dominant society (this would have to be verified at the beginning of the study), we could try to find out how members of the category classify other drinkers and what indicators they use to identify the people they include in these categories. We might find that their taxonomies include a category corresponding to a construct "alcohol addict." If so, we would investigate the criteria they use to identify themselves or others as members of this category. The underlying assumption might be described as "it takes one to know one." The motivation is not mere idle curiosity about how people divide up their worlds, though that is interesting in itself. It is conceivable that drinkers might know something about identifying "alcohol addicts" (assuming we find that they use such a category) which would be useful in diagnosis and perhaps even in treatment.

Physicians and many other scientists might dismiss such a possibility as absurd. After all, we do not ask one schizophrenic how he recognizes another one. However, recent experimental evidence suggests that this approach might be instructive. In an experiment reported by Rosenhan (166), 12 volunteers gained admission to mental hospitals merely by stating they had heard hollow voices. They stopped feigning these abnormal symptoms as soon as they were admitted, but the hospital staff did not discover they had entered under false pretenses. However, 35 of 188 real patients did detect that the pseudopatients were somehow different. They said, "You're not crazy. You're a journalist, or a professor. You're checking up on the hospital." In light of these findings, it is not possible to rule out that "alcohol addicts" might teach physicians something about identifying and classifying the people who qualify for this label. Jellinek, at any rate, was willing to learn from alcoholics.

Ethnoscience studies might, on the other hand, discover that most dominant-society drinkers' taxonomies of "drinkers" do not include a category "alcohol addict." (Those who do use the category might have obtained it by diffusion from medical practitioners or other groups, and may have only superficially integrated it into their conceptual maps.) In view of our experience with the label thus far, absence of the category "alcohol addict" from the world view of "drinkers" might be interpreted as a tribute to their folk wisdom, a demonstration that they may know more about drinkers than the "experts." Such a finding, however interpreted, would be of great interest. But more interesting still would be the alternative categories involved.

Both "medical practitioners" and "drinkers" are dominant-society groups. A case could be made for beginning ethnoscience studies of drinking in a group somewhat removed from the dominant society. Until empirical data to the contrary are obtained, it is necessary to assume that for such groups "alcohol addiction" is an a priori construct—an etic category derived from American dominant-society preconceptions. A group such as American Indians, who are partly within and partly outside the dominant society, would provide a means of testing this hypothesis. If the concept were absent in a group as similar to the dominant society as Indians (compared to African Bushmen, for example), this would suggest an even smaller likelihood of encountering the construct in less similar cultural groups.

Given the difficulty of achieving laboratory conditions in studies of human behavior, alcohol-related or otherwise, possible differential incidence of manifestations such as those interpreted by the dominant society as diagnostic of a category "alcohol addict" might provide the best substitute available. The possibility that "alcohol addiction" may be rare among American Indians, for example, provides an opportunity to study the concept from a fresh perspective. Presumably observers would be somewhat less "of the world" of Indians than of groups more similar to their own; thus, they might more easily recognize their preconceptions as such. Trying to discover whether "alcohol addiction" really is rare among Indians might stimulate observers to analyze dominant-society criteria for this construct more critically than if they began with their own culture.

If it were discovered that the folk category "alcohol addict" does exist among Indians, comparison of criteria for inclusion in the category between Indians and dominant-society members might pinpoint behavioral differences which have been overlooked in the past. On the other hand, if the construct "alcohol addict" is not part of the conceptual maps of Indians, the categories of drinkers that were discovered to exist and the diagnostic clues for them might point to thus far undetected characteristics of the group which would be helpful in identifying and in dealing with the group's alcohol-associated problems.

Furthermore, if the construct "alcohol addiction" were absent among Indians and, in addition, it were verified that manifestations interpreted by the dominant society as symptomatic of "alcohol addiction" were also absent, this might provide a rare framework for study of the interaction between behavior and world view. Whatever the initial target population, documentation of the drinking behavior and beliefs of insiders would add valuable perspective to alcohol studies.

APPENDIX

Indian Groups Covered in the Literature Cited, by Culture Area*

CULTURE AREA, GROUP	REFERENCE	ERA† H	M	COMMUNITY TYPE† R	N	U	?
Arctic Coast							
Aleut of Nikolski	Berreman (10)		√	√			
Eskimo & Indians of Kaktovik, Barrow, Wainwright	Chance (20, 21)		√	√			
Eskimo of Aklavik	Clairmont (22, 23)		√	√			
Eskimo of Frobisher Bay	Honigmanns (70)		√		√		
Eskimo, Indians & other natives of Inuvik	Honigmann (231, 232) Honigmanns (234)	√	√		√		
Eskimo, Indians & other natives of Mackenzie Delta	Honigmanns (69, 233)		√		√		
Subarctic							
Vunta Kutchin of Old Crow	Balikci (7)		√	√			
Kaska of "Delio"	Honigmanns (68)		√	√			
Chipewyan, Eskimo & other natives of Churchill, Manitoba	Koolage (99)		√	√			
Naskapi	Robbins (162), Horton (71)		√	√	√		
Northwest Coast	Lemert (107), Howay (72)	√	√	√			
Bella Coola	McIlwraith (122)	√	√	√			
3 Salish tribes (Homalthko, Sliammon and Tlahoose)	Lemert (108)	√	√	√			
Kwakiutl of Guilford Island	Rohner & Rohner (165)		√	√			
Plateau							
Klamath	Du Toit (38)		√	√			
Colville Reservation, Confederated tribes	Indian Workshop (224)		√	√			
Plains							
Kiowa Apache	Freeman (52)		√	√			
Oglala Sioux	Maynard (129), Mindell (237)		√	√			

* Based on Driver and Massey (37).
† H = historical, M = modern; R = reservation or Indian nonurban, N = nonurban, mixed, U = urban, ? = unknown.

CULTURE AREA, GROUP	REFERENCE	ERA † H M		COMMUNITY TYPE † R N U ?			
Prairies							
Sioux							
Cheyenne River, Pineridge, Rosebud, Standing Rock (misc.)	Medicine (130)	✓	✓				
Standing Rock	Whittaker (212, 213)	✓	✓				
Yankton, living in Yankton, also Dakota	White (210), Hurt (73), Hurt & Brown (74)	✓	✓			✓	
Indians in Omaha (Omaha, Winnebago, Ponca, S. Dakota Sioux)	Kuttner & Lorincz (103)		✓		✓		
Kansas Territory	Frederickson (51)	✓					
Menomini of Zoar ("conservatives")	Slotkin (175)		✓	✓			
Osage	LaBarre (104)		✓	✓			
Potawatomi of "Whitehorse"	Hamer (58, 59)	✓	✓	✓			
East							
Iroquois	Carpenter (19)	✓					
Onandaga County, N.Y.	Gabe et al. (53)		✓	✓	✓	✓	
Desert							
Duck Valley Reservation, Nevada (Northern Paiute, Shoshoni)	Manning (125)		✓	✓			
Indians of Nevada; court and welfare referrals, inmates	Kilen (236)		✓	✓	✓	✓	
Uintah-Ouray Northern Ute	Collins (25), Slater (238, 239)		✓	✓	✓		
Southern Ute, triethnic town in So. Colorado	Graves (56), Jessor (86), Jessor et al. (87)		✓		✓		
Oasis							
Apache							
"of Arizona"	Bourke (11)	✓					
Jicarilla	Jicarilla Alcohol Project (88)		✓	✓			
Mescalero	Bollinger & Starkey (227)		✓	✓			
	Boyer (14)		✓	✓			
	Curley (27)		✓	✓			
White Mountain	Levy & Kunitz (111) Kunitz et al. (102)	✓	✓	✓			

† H = historical, M = modern; R = reservation or Indian nonurban, N = nonurban, mixed, U = urban, ? = unknown.

CULTURE AREA, GROUP	REFERENCE	ERA†		COMMUNITY TYPE†			
		H	M	R	N	U	?
Oasis (Cont.)							
Navaho	Levy & Kunitz (112, 113)	√	√	√	√		
	Levy et al. (115)	√	√	√	√		
USPHS hospital & clinic patients, Phoenix & Window Rock	Kunitz et al. (102)	√	√	√	√		
USPHS hospital patients of Navaho Reservation, successful suicides, Navaho police records and historical sources	Kunitz et al. (101)	√	√	√	√		
	Levy (110)	√	√	√			
120 patients of "A Community Treatment Program for Navaho Problem Drinkers," recruited on the basis of 10 arrests	Ferguson (46, 47, 48) Henderson (64, 65)		√	√	√		
Ramah Navaho (data from Harvard Values Study)	Geertz (230)	√	√				
"Rimrock" Navaho (Ramah Navaho), HVS	Heath (62)	√	√				
"Rimrock" Navaho, plus data from "personal communications with a number of Navahos and knowledgeable Anglos.... 1953 to 1961.... Regional variation undoubtedly persists, but seems relatively unimportant" (63, *p. 128*)	Heath (63)	√	√				
Migrants to Denver	Graves (57), Snyder (178)		√			√	
200 disulfiram patients, Ft. Defiance Hospital	Savard (169), Szuter et al. (187)		√	√			
Psychiatric hospital patients	Kaplan & Johnson (89), Kaplan (235)		√	√			
Hopi	Kunitz et al. (101, 102)	√	√	√	√		
	Levy & Kunitz (112, 113)	√	√	√	√		
	Horton (71)	√	√	√			
Zuni	Geertz (230), Horton (71)	√	√	√			

† H = historical, M = modern; R = reservation or Indian nonurban, N = nonurban, mixed, U = urban, ? = unknown.

CULTURE AREA, GROUP	REFERENCE	ERA†		COMMUNITY TYPE†			
		H	M	R	N	U	?
Oasis (Cont.)							
"New Mexico Tribes" Apache, Pueblo, Navajo, Ute patients of the Community Mental Health program	Andre (226)		√	√			
Indians served by New Mexico Commission on Alcoholism	Toler (191), Werner (209)		√	√	√	√	
Miscellaneous groups, predominantly Oasis Phoenix Indian Hospital autopsies: Pima, Papago, Apache = 78%	Reichenbach (160)		√	√			
Phoenix Indian Hospital patients over age 15 years: Pima, Apache, Navaho, Papago = 74%	Sievers (174)		√	√			
Mohave	Devereux (33)	√	√	√			
"Indians," probably Oasis only	McKinley (123); also quoting Wellman and Werner		√	√			
Miscellaneous (several culture areas combined)							
British Columbia (Yukon & Mackenzie Subarctic, Northwest Coast, Plateau)	Hawthorne et al. (61)		√	√	√	√	
Indians of Washington State (Northwest Coast, Plateau)	Clark (24)	√					
Indians of the American Frontier	Winkler (216)	√		√			
36 Federal prison inmates: Sioux (Prairie) and Apache (Oasis) = 50%	Baker (5)		√				√
Indians on Ottawa's Skid Row: Cree, Blackfoot, Chipewyan, Sarcee, Hare, Slave, Iroquoian, Kootenayan, Northwest Coast, Eskimo	Brody (16)		√			√	

† H = historical, M = modern; R = reservation or Indian nonurban, N = nonurban, mixed, U = urban, ? = unknown.

		ERA †		COMMUNITY TYPE †		
CULTURE AREA, GROUP	REFERENCE	H	M	R	N	U ?

Miscellaneous (Cont.)

CULTURE AREA, GROUP	REFERENCE	H	M	R	N	U	?
Indians of Chicago (uptown), St. Augustine's Center for American Indians of various tribal origins. Also quotes and makes some generalizations about "Indians" and individual groups	Littman (117)		√			√	
Indians of Chicago, psychiatric outpatient clinic for alcoholics, various tribal origins	Littman (116)		√			√	
Indians in San Francisco, various tribal origins	Swett (241)		√			√	
"Indians" of North America	Akwesasne Notes (223),		√				√
	American Indian workshop (222)		√				√
	Dozier (36)	√	√	√	√	√	
	Fahy & Muschenheim (40)		√	√	√	√	
	Tax, quoted by Geyer (54)		√				√
	Martinez (127)	√	√				
	MacAndrew & Edgerton (121)	√	√	√	√	√	
	Reifel (161)		√	√			
	Sanchez (168)	√	√	√			
	Suarez (185)		√	√			
	U.S. H.E.W. (198)		√	√	√	√	
High-school students	Boyce (13)		√	√			
Certain Canadian reserves, only?	Dailey (28)	√	√	√			
Arrested	von Hentig (66)	√					√
Based mostly on Menomini, Chippewa, Winnebago, Walker River Paiutes and Eastern Pueblos, but generalizes about Indians as a whole	Spindlers (181)		√	√	√		
National data on all Indians, plus data on some individual groups: San Carlos Apache, Jicarilla Apache, Navaho, Colorado Utes, Southern Ute, Ute Mountain Ute, United Pueblo Agency	Stewart (184)		√	√	√	√	

† H = historical, M = modern; R = reservation or Indian nonurban, N = nonurban, mixed, U = urban, ? = unknown.

CULTURE AREA, GROUP	REFERENCE	ERA †		COMMUNITY TYPE †			
		H	M	R	N	U	?
Miscellaneous (Cont.)							
New France (historical)	Belmont (9), Dailey (29), Delanglez (32), Salone (167), Thwaites (190), Vachon (203)	✓		✓			
Unknown (*Anonymous Indian communities*)	Keneally (97) also quoting Krutz, B.I.A. official quoted by Officer (152)	✓		✓			

† H = historical, M = modern; R = reservation or Indian nonurban, N = nonurban, mixed, U = urban, ? = unknown.

BIBLIOGRAPHY
Published Documents

1. ABERLE, D. F. [anthropologist] The peyote religion among the Navaho. (Viking Fund Publications in Anthropology, No. 42.) Chicago; Aldine; 1966.

2. BACON, M. K., BARRY, H., 3d, BUCHWALD, C., CHILD, I. L. and SNYDER, C. R. [4 psychologists, 1 sociologist] A cross-cultural study of drinking. Quart. J. Stud. Alc., Suppl. No. 3, 1965.

3. BACON, S. D. [sociologist] Alcoholics do not drink. Ann. Amer. Acad. polit. social Sci. 315: 55–64, 1958.

4. BACON, S. D. The process of addiction to alcohol; social aspects. Quart. J. Stud. Alc. 34: 1–27, 1973.

5. BAKER, J. L. [M.D.] Indians, alcohol and homicide. J. social Ther. 5: 270–275, 1959. [Sioux, Apache, various other Indian Federal prison inmates]

6. BALES, R. F. [sociologist] Cultural differences in rates of alcoholism. Quart. J. Stud. Alc. 6: 480–499, 1946.

7. BALIKCI, A. [anthropologist] Bad friends. Hum. Organiz. 27: 191–199, 1968. [Vunta Kutchin Indians of Old Crow, Yukon]

8. BARNETT, M. L. [anthropologist] Alcoholism in the Cantonese of New York City; an anthropological study. In: DIETHELM, O., ed. Etiology of chronic alcoholism. Springfield, IL; Thomas; 1955.

9. BELMONT, F. V. DE [Catholic priest] The history of brandy in Canada. Mid-America 34: 42–63, 1952. (First published in French in 1840 from an undated manuscript of the early 1700s: Histoire de l'Eau-de-Vie en Canada.) [Indians of New France]

10. BERREMAN, G. D. [anthropologist] Drinking patterns of the Aleuts. Quart. J. Stud. Alc. 17: 503–514, 1956. [Nikolski Aleuts]

11. BOURKE, J. G. [Captain, U.S. Army] Distillation by early American Indians. Amer. Anthrop. 7: 297–299, 1894. [Includes "Apaches of Arizona"]

12. BOWMAN, K. M. and JELLINEK, E. M. [psychiatrist and biometrician] Alcohol addiction and its treatment. Quart. J. Stud. Alc. 2: 98–176, 1941.

13. BOYCE, G. A. [superintendent, Indian school] Alcohol and American Indian students. Washington, DC; U.S. Bureau of Indian Affairs; 1965. [North American Indian high-school students]

14. BOYER, L. B. [psychiatrist] Psychological problems of a group of Apache; alcoholic hallucinosis and latent homosexuality among typical men. Pp. 203–277. In: MUENSTENRBERGER, W. and AXELRAD, S., eds. The psychoanalytic study of society. Vol. 3. New York; International Universities Press; 1964. [Mescalero]

15. BRENNER, B. [sociologist] Estimating the prevalence of alcoholism; toward a modification of the Jellinek formula. Quart. J. Stud. Alc. 20: 255–260, 1959.

16. BRODY, H. [anthropologist] Indians on Skid Row. (NCRC 70–2) Ottawa; Canadian Dept. of Indian Affairs and Northern Development; 1971.

139

17. CAHALAN, D. [social psychologist] Problem drinkers; a national survey. San Francisco; Jossey-Bass; 1970.

18. CAHALAN, D., CISIN, I. H. and CROSSLEY, H. M. [social psychologist, sociologist, specialist in survey research] American drinking practices; a national study of drinking behavior and attitudes. (Rutgers Center of Alcohol Studies, Monogr. No. 6.) New Brunswick, NJ; 1969.

19. CARPENTER, E. S. [anthropologist] Alcohol in the Iroquois dream quest. Amer. J. Psychiat. 116: 148–151, 1959.

20. CHANCE, N. A. [anthropologist] Culture change and integration; an Eskimo example. Amer. Anthrop. 62: 1028–1044, 1960.

21. CHANCE, N. A. Eskimo of North Alaska; case studies in cultural anthropology. New York; Holt, Rinehart & Winston; 1966. [Eskimo of Kaktovik]

22. CLAIRMONT, D. H. J. [anthropologist] Notes on the drinking behaviour of the Eskimos and Indians in the Aklavik area; a preliminary report. (NCRC 62–4.) Ottawa; Canadian Dept. of Northern Affairs and National Resources; 1962.

23. CLAIRMONT, D. H. J. Deviance among Indian Eskimos in Aklavik, N. W. T. (NCRC 63–9.) Ottawa; Canadian Dept. of Northern Affairs and National Resources; 1963.

24. CLARK, N. H. [historian] The dry years; prohibition and social change in Washington. Seattle; University of Washington Press; 1965. [Includes Indians of Washington State]

25. COLLINS, T. W. [anthropologist] The Northern Ute economic development program; social and cultural dimensions. Ph.D. dissertation, University of Colorado; 1971.

26. COOPERATIVE COMMISSION ON THE STUDY OF ALCOHOLISM. Alcohol problems; a report to the nation by the Cooperative Commission on the Study of Alcoholism. Prepared by T. F. A. PLAUT. New York; Oxford University Press; 1967.

27. CURLEY, R. T. [sociologist] Drinking patterns of the Mescalero Apache. Quart. J. Stud. Alc. 28: 116–131, 1967.

28. DAILEY, R. C. [anthropologist] Alcohol and the North American Indian; implications for the management of problems. Sel. Pap. 17th Annu. Mtg N. Amer. Ass. Alcsm Programs, pp. 22–28, 1967.

29. DAILEY, R. C. The role of alcohol among North American Indian tribes as reported in the Jesuit relations. Anthropologica 10: 45–57, 1968.

30. DAVIES, D. L. [psychiatrist] Normal drinking in recovered alcohol addicts. Quart. J. Stud. Alc. 23: 94–104, 1962.

31. DAVIS, V. E. and WALSH, M. J. [biochemists] Alcohol, amines and alkaloids; a possible biochemical basis for alcohol addiction. Science 167: 1005–1006, 1970.

32. DELANGLEZ, J. [historian] Frotenac and the Jesuits. Chicago; Institute of Jesuit History; 1939.

33. DEVEREUX, G. [anthropologist] The function of alcohol in Mohave society. Quart. J. Stud. Alc. 9: 207–251, 1948.

34. DIETHELM, O. [psychiatrist] Research in chronic alcoholism. In: Diethelm, O., ed. Etiology of chronic alcoholism. Springfield, IL; Thomas; 1955.

35. DOUGLASS, W. G. and NOEL, G. N. Reports of cases determined in the Supreme Court of the State of Nevada during 1906 and 1907. *Vol.* 29. Carson City; State Printing Office; 1908.

36. DOZIER, E. P. [anthropologist] Problem drinking among American Indians; the role of sociocultural deprivation. Quart. J. Stud. Alc. 27: 72–87, 1966.

37. DRIVER, H. E. and MASSEY, W. C. [anthropologists] Comparative studies of North American Indians. Trans. Amer. phil. Soc. 47: 165–456, 1957.

38. DU TOIT, B. M. [anthropologist] Substitution, a process in culture change. Hum. Organiz. 23: 16–23, 1964. [Klamath]

39. EDDY, N. B., HALBACH, H., ISBELL, H. and SIEVERS, M. H. [M.D.s] Drug dependence; its significance and characteristics. Bull. World Hlth Org. 32: 721–733 1965.

40. FAHY, A. and MUSCHENHEIM, C. [? and M.D.] Third national conference on American Indian health. J. Amer. med. Ass. 194: 1093–1096, 1965. [North American Indians, reservation]

41. FALLDING, H. [sociologist] The source and burden of civilization illustrated in the use of alcohol. Quart. J. Stud. Alc. 25: 714–724, 1964.

42. FEDERAL BUREAU OF INVESTIGATION. Uniform crime reports for the United States—1960. U.S. Department of Justice. Washington, DC; U.S. Govt Print. Off.; 1961.

43. FEDERAL BUREAU OF INVESTIGATION. Uniform crime reporting handbook. U.S. Department of Justice. Washington, DC; U.S. Govt Print. Off.; 1966.

44. FEDERAL BUREAU OF INVESTIGATION. Uniform crime reports for the United States—1970. U.S. Department of Justice. Washington, DC; U.S. Govt Print. Off.; 1971.

45. FENNA, D., MIX, L., SCHAEFER, D. and GILBERT, J. A. L. [biochemists] Ethanol metabolism in various racial groups. Canad. med. Ass. J. 105: 472–475, 1971.

46. FERGUSON, F. N. [anthropologist] The Navaho drinker as an individual; implications of the National Institute of Mental Health Gallup Treatment Program Results. In: Utah School of Alcohol Studies, 1967 (202).

47. FERGUSON, F. N. Navaho drinking; some tentative hypotheses. Hum. Organiz. 27: 159–167, 1968.

48. FERGUSON, F. N. A treatment program for Navaho alcoholics; results after 4 years. Quart. J. Stud. Alc. 31: 898–919, 1970.

49. FIELD, P. B. [psychologist] A new cross-cultural study of drunkenness. Pp. 48–74. In: PITTMAN, D. J. and SNYDER, C. R., eds. Society, culture, and drinking patterns. New York; Wiley; 1962.

50. FINGARETTE, H. [lawyer] The perils of Powell; in search of a factual foundation for the "disease concept of alcoholism." Harvard Law Rev. 83: 793–812, 1970.

51. FREDERICKSON, O. F. [historian] The liquor question among the Indian tribes in Kansas, 1804–1881. Bull. Univ. Kans., humanist. Stud., No. 4, 1932.

52. FREEMAN, D. M. [M.D.] Adolescent crises of the Kiowa-Apache Indian

male. Pp. 157–204. In: Brody, E. B., ed. Minority group adolescents in the United States. Baltimore; Williams & Wilkins; 1968.

53. Gabe, R. C., Phelps, G. H. and Ruck, J. A. [graduate students in social work] An exploratory study of the incidence of alcohol-related arrests among American Indians of Onondaga County, New York. Master's thesis, Syracuse University; 1968.

54. Geyer, G. A. [journalist] Why the Indian loses out. Chicago Daily News, 29 January 1963.

55. Goodenough, W. H. [anthropologist] Description and comparison in cultural anthropology. Chicago; Aldine; 1970.

56. Graves, T. D. [anthropologist] Acculturation, access, and alcohol in a tri-ethnic community. Amer. Anthrop. 69: 306–321, 1967. [Ute]

57. Graves, T. D. The personal adjustment of Navajo Indian migrants to Denver, Colorado. Amer. Anthrop. 72: 35–54, 1970.

58. Hamer, J. H. [anthropologist] Acculturation stress and the functions of alcohol among the Forest Potawatomi. Quart. J. Stud. Alc. 26: 285–302, 1965.

59. Hamer, J. H. Guardian spirits, alcohol, and cultural defense mechanisms. Anthropologica 11: 215–241, 1969. [Forest Potawatomi]

60. Harris, F. R. and Harris, L. [U.S. Senator and his wife who is part-Comanche] Indian health. In: Sources—a Blue Cross report on the health problems of the poor. Chicago; 1968. Cit. Littman (117).

61. Hawthorn, H. B., Belshaw, C. S. and Jamieson, S. M. [anthropologists] The Indians of British Columbia and alcohol. Alc. Rev., B.C. 2: 10–14, 1957.

62. Heath, D. B. [anthropologist] Alcohol in a Navajo community. A.B. thesis, Harvard College; 1952.

63. Heath, D. B. Prohibition and post-repeal drinking patterns among the Navaho. Quart. J. Stud. Alc. 25: 119–135, 1964.

64. Henderson, N. B. [psychologist] Community treatment plan for Navaho problem drinkers. In: Utah School of Alcohol Studies, 1965 (202).

65. Henderson, N. B. Cross-cultural action research; some limitations, advantages and problems. J. social Psychol. 73: 61–70, 1967. [Zuni, Navaho]

66. Hentig, H. v. [lawyer] The delinquency of the American Indian. J. crim. Law Criminol. 36: 75–84, 1945. [North American Indians]

67. Honigmann, J. J. [anthropologist] Culture and ethos of Kaska society. (Yale University Publications in Anthropology, No. 40.) New Haven; 1949.

68. Honigmann, J. J. and Honigmann, I. Drinking in an Indian–white community. Quart. J. Stud. Alc. 5: 575–619, 1945. [Kaska]

69. Honigmann, J. J. and Honigmann, I. Eskimo townsmen. Ottawa; Canadian Centre for Anthropology, University of Ottawa; 1965. [Mackenzie Delta]

70. Honigmann, J. J. and Honigmann, I. How Baffin Island Eskimo have learned to use alcohol. Social Forces 44: 73–83, 1965. [Frobisher Bay]

71. Horton, D. [anthropologist] The function of alcohol in primitive societies; a cross-cultural study. Quart. J. Stud. Alc. 4: 199–320, 1943. [includes Naskapi, Navaho, Papago, Zuni]

72. HOWAY, F. W. [historian] The introduction of intoxicating liquors amongst the Indians of the Northwest Coast. B.C. hist. Quart. **6**: 157–169, 1942.

73. HURT, W. R. [anthropologist] The urbanization of the Yankton Indians. Hum. Organiz. **20**: 226–231, 1962.

74. HURT, W. R. and BROWN, R. M. [anthropologist and ?] Social drinking patterns of the Yankton Sioux. Hum. Organiz. **24**: 222–230, 1965. [Indians of Yankton, SD, and Dakota branch of the Sioux, parental stock of the Indians of Yankton]

75. INDIAN HEALTH SERVICE TASK FORCE ON ALCOHOLISM. Alcoholism; a high priority health problem. Section 1. Washington, DC; U.S. Public Health Service, Indian Health Service; 1969. [North American Indians]

76. INDIAN HEALTH SERVICE TASK FORCE ON ALCOHOLISM. Alcoholism; a high priority health problem. Section 2. Washington, DC; U.S. Public Health Service, Indian Health Service; 1970. [North American Indians]

77. JACKSON, J. K. [sociologist] The definition and measurement of alcoholism; H-technique scales of preoccupation with alcohol and psychological involvement. Quart. J. Stud. Alc. **18**: 240–262, 1957.

78. JELLINEK, E. M. [biometrician] Phases in the drinking history of alcoholics; analysis of a survey conducted by the Grapevine, official organ of Alcoholics Anonymous. Quart. J. Stud. Alc. **7**: 1–88, 1946.

79. JELLINEK, E. M. Recent trends in alcoholism and in alcohol consumption. Quart. J. Stud. Alc. **8**: 1–42, 1947.

80. JELLINEK, E. M. The estimate of the number of alcoholics in the U.S.A. for 1949 in the light of the sixth revision of the international lists of causes of death. Quart. J. Stud. Alc. **13**: 215–218, 1949.

81. JELLINEK, E. M. Phases of alcohol addiction. Quart. J. Stud. Alc. **13**: 673–684, 1952.

82. JELLINEK, E. M. The world and its bottle. World Hlth, Geneva **10**: 4–6, 1957.

83. JELLINEK, E. M. Estimating the prevalence of alcoholism; modified values in the Jellinek formula and an alternative approach. Quart. J. Stud. Alc. **20**: 261–269, 1959.

84. JELLINEK, E. M. The disease concept of alcoholism. Highland Park, NJ; Hillhouse; 1960.

85. JELLINEK, E. M. Alcoholism, a genus and some of its species. Canad. med. Ass. J. **83**: 1341–1345, 1960.

86. JESSOR, R. [psychologist] Toward a social psychology of excessive alcohol use. Pp. 60–79. In: SNYDER, C. R. and SCHWEITZER, D. R., eds. Proceedings of the Research Sociologists' Conference on Alcohol Problems. Carbondale, IL; Southern Illinois University; 1964.

87. JESSOR, R., GRAVES, T. D., HANSON, R. C., and JESSOR, S. L. [2 psychologists, 1 anthropologist, 1 sociologist] Society, personality and deviant behavior; a study of a tri-ethnic community. New York; Holt, Rinehart & Winston; 1968. [Ute]

88. JICARILLA APACHE ALCOHOLISM PROJECT. Project for the treatment and prevention of alcoholism on the Jicarilla reservation. Dulce, NM; 1969. [Mimeographed.]

89. KAPLAN, B. and JOHNSON, D. [anthropologists] The social meaning of Navajo psychopathology and psychotherapy. Pp. 203–229. In: KIEV, A., ed. Magic, faith and healing. New York; Free Press; 1964.

90. KELLER, M. [documentalist, editor] Alcoholism; nature and extent of the problem. Ann. Amer. Acad. polit. social Sci. 315: 1–11, 1958.

91. KELLER, M. The definition of alcoholism and the estimation of its prevalence. Pp. 310–329. In: PITTMAN, D. J. and SNYDER, C. R., eds. Society, culture, and drinking patterns. New York; Wiley; 1962.

92. KELLER, M. Alcoholism as disability. Pp. 28–36. In: BERKOWITZ, M., ed. Estimating rehabilitation needs, a conference on planning for vocational rehabilitation. New Brunswick, NJ; Bureau of Economic Research, Rutgers University; 1967.

93. KELLER, M. Some views on the nature of addiction. The E. M. Jellinek memorial lecture, presented at the 15th International Institute on the Prevention and Treatment of Alcoholism, Budapest, 9 June 1969. Lausanne; International Bureau on Alcoholism and Drug Addiction; 1969.

94. KELLER, M. On the loss-of-control phenomenon in alcoholism. Brit. J. Addict. 67: 153–166, 1972.

95. KELLER, M. and McCORMICK, M. [documentalist and writer] A dictionary of words about alcohol. New Brunswick, NJ; Rutgers Center of Alcohol Studies; 1968.

96. KELLER, M. and SEELEY, J. R. [documentalist and sociologist] The alcohol language; with a selected vocabulary. Toronto; University of Toronto Press; 1958.

97. KENEALLY, H., JR. [health educator] The first step. (7 pp.) In: Utah School of Alcohol Studies, 1966 (202). [anonymous Indian community]

98. KING, L. S. [M.D., editor] How does a pathologist make a diagnosis? Arch. Path. 84: 331–333, 1967.

99. KOOLAGE, W. W., JR. [anthropologist] Adaptation of Chipewyan Indians and other persons of native background in Churchill, Manitoba. Ph.D. dissertation, University of North Carolina; 1970.

100. KUNITZ, S. J. [M.D.] Navajo drinking patterns. Ph.D. dissertation, Yale University; 1970.

101. KUNITZ, S. J., LEVY, J. E. and EVERETT, M. [M.D., anthropologists] Alcoholic cirrhosis among the Navaho. Quart. J. Stud. Alc. 30: 672–685, 1969.

102. KUNITZ, S. J., LEVY, J. E., ODOROFF, C. L. and BOLLINGER, J. [M.D., anthropologist, M.D., medical student] The epidemiology of alcoholic cirrhosis in two southwestern Indian tribes. Quart. J. Stud. Alc. 32: 706–720, 1971.

103. KUTTNER, R. E. and LORINCZ, A. B. [biochemist, M.D.] Alcoholism and addiction in urbanized Sioux Indians. Ment. Hyg., Lond. 51: 530–542, 1967. [Hopi also]

104. LABARRE, W. [anthropologist] A cultist drug-addiction in an Indian alcoholic. Bull. Menninger Clin. 5: 40–46, 1941. [Osage]

105. LELAND, J. [anthropologist] Alcohol addiction among North American Indians. M.A. thesis, University of Nevada; 1972.

106. LEMERE, F. [psychiatrist] What causes alcoholism. J. clin. exp. Psychopath. 17: 202–206, 1956.

107. LEMERT, E. M. [anthropologist] Alcohol and the Northwest Coast Indians. Univ. Calif. Publ. Cult. Soc. 2: 303–406, 1954.

108. LEMERT, E. M. The use of alcohol in three Salish Indian tribes. Quart. J. Stud. Alc. 19: 90–107, 1958.

109. LESTER, D. [biochemist] Self-selection of alcohol by animals, human variation and the etiology of alcoholism; a critical review. Quart. J. Stud. Alc. 27: 395–438, 1966.

110. LEVY, J. E. [anthropologist] Navajo suicide. Hum. Organiz. 24: 308–318, 1965.

111. LEVY, J. E. and KUNITZ, S. J. [anthropologist and M.D.] Notes on some White Mountain Apache social pathologies. Plateau 42: 11–19, 1969.

112. LEVY, J. E. and KUNITZ, S. J. Indian reservations, anomie and social pathologies. Sthwest. J. Anthrop. 27: 97–128, 1971.

113. LEVY, J. E. and KUNITZ, S. J. Indian drinking; problems of data collection and interpretation. Proc. 1st Annu. Alcsm Conf. NIAAA, pp. 217–236, 1973.

114. LEVY, J. E. and KUNITZ, S. J. Indian drinking; Navajo practices and Anglo-American theories. New York; Wiley; 1974.

115. LEVY, J. E., KUNITZ, S. J. and EVERETT, M. [anthropologist, M.D. and anthropologist] Navajo criminal homicide. Sthwest. J. Anthrop. 25: 124–152, 1969.

116. LITTMAN, G. [social worker] Some observations on drinking among American Indians in Chicago. Pp. 67–78. In: Selected Papers Presented at the 27th International Congress on Alcohol and Alcoholism, Frankfurt-am-Main, 1964. Vol. 1. Lausanne; International Bureau Against Alcoholism; 1965.

117. LITTMAN, G. Alcoholism, illness, and social pathology among American Indians in transition. Amer. J. publ. Hlth 60: 1769-1787, 1970. [Indians of Chicago]

118. LOEB, E. M. Primitive intoxicants. Quart. J. Stud. Alc. 4: 387–398, 1943.

119. LOFLAND, J. F. and LEJEUNE, R. A. [sociologists] Initial interaction of newcomers in Alcoholics Anonymous; a field experiment in class symbols and socialization. Social Probl. 8: 102–111, 1960.

120. MACANDREW, C. [psychologist] On the notion that certain persons who are given to frequent drunkenness suffer from a disease called alcoholism. In: PLOG, S. C. and EDGERTON, R. B., eds. Changing perspectives in mental illness. New York; Holt, Rinehart & Winston; 1969.

121. MACANDREW, C. and EDGERTON, R. B. [psychologist, anthropologist] Drunken comportment; a social explanation. Chicago; Aldine; 1969. [North American Indians]

122. MCILWRAITH, T. F. [anthropologist] The Bella Coola Indians. 3 vol. Toronto; University of Toronto Press; 1948.

123. MCKINLEY, F. I. [assistant director, Indian Education Center, Arizona State University] An overview of Indian alcoholism. Pp. 30–34. In: Annual report. Scottsdale, AZ; Southwest Indian Alcoholism Council; 1965. [North American Indians, probably Oasis, only]

124. MANDELBAUM, D. G. [anthropologist] Alcohol and culture. Curr. Anthrop. 6: 281–293, 1965. [includes South American Indians]

125. MANNING, L. [social worker, tribal member] Step-by-step report of how an A.A. program began in a northern Nevada Indian reservation. In: Utah School of Alcohol Studies, 1963 (202). [Shoshoni-Northern Paiute]

126. MARCONI-T., J. [psychiatrist] The concept of alcoholism. Quart. J. Stud. Alc. 20: 216–235, 1959.

127. MARTINEZ, F. H. [field representative, New Mexico Commission on Alcoholism] Extent and scope of Indian drinking problems. Salt Lake City; Utah Committee on Alcoholism; 1968. [Mimeographed.] [North American Indians, probably Oasis only]

128. MAXWELL, M. A. [sociologist] Alcoholics Anonymous; an interpretation. Pp. 577–585. In: PITTMAN, D. J. and SNYDER, C. R., eds. Society, culture, and drinking patterns. New York; Wiley; 1962.

129. MAYNARD, E. [anthropologist] Drinking as part of an adjustment syndrome among the Oglala Sioux. Parts I and II. Pine Ridge Res. Bull., No. 9, pp. 35–51, 1969.

130. MEDICINE, B. [anthropologist, Sioux tribal member] The changing Dakota family and the stresses therein. Pine Ridge Res. Bull., No. 9, pp. 1–20, 1969.

131. MEIER, H. C. [sociologist] Three ethnic groups in a Southwestern community. M.A. thesis, University of Colorado; 1951. [Ute]

132. MELLO, N. K., McNAMEE, H. B. and MENDELSON, J. H. [psychologist, 2 psychiatrists] Drinking patterns of chronic alcoholics; gambling and motivation for alcohol. Pp. 83–118. In: COLE, J. O., ed. Clinical research in alcoholism. (Psychiatric Research Rep., No. 24.) Washington, DC; American Psychiatric Association; 1968.

133. MELLO, N. K. and MENDELSON, J. H. Experimentally induced intoxication in alcoholics; a comparison between programmed and spontaneous drinking. J. Pharmacol. 173: 101–116, 1970.

134. MENDELSON, J. H. [psychiatrist] Alcoholism—an overview. Pp. 17–24. In: Social welfare and alcoholism; conference proceedings. Washington, DC; U.S. Dept. of Health, Education, and Welfare; 1968.

135. MENDELSON, J. H., MELLO, N. K. and SOLOMON, P. [psychiatrist, psychologist, and psychiatrist] Small group drinking behavior; an experimental study of chronic alcoholics. Res. Publ. nerv. ment. Dis. 46: 399–430, 1968.

136. MERRY, J. [psychiatrist] The "loss of control" myth. Lancet 1: 1257–1258, 1966.

137. MOORE, R. A. [psychiatrist] Alcoholism in Japan. Quart. J. Stud. Alc. 25: 142–150, 1964.

138. MOORE, R. A.; DEWES, P. B.; DUMONT, M. P.; ROOM, R. Comment on "The alcohologist's addiction." Quart. J. Stud. Alc. 33: 1043–1059, 1972.

139. MORSIER, G. DE and FELDMAN, H. [M.D.s] Le traitement de l'alcoolisme par l'apomorphine; étude de 500 cas. Schweiz. Arch. Neurol. Psychiat. 70: 434–440, 1952.

140. MOSCOW, H. A., PENNINGTON, R. C. and KNISELEY, M. H. [anatomists] Alcohol, sludge and hypoxic areas of nervous system, liver and heart. Microvasc. Res. 1: 174–185, 1968.

141. MULFORD, H. A. [sociologist] Drinking and deviant behavior, U.S.A., 1963. Quart. J. Stud. Alc. 25: 634–650, 1964.

142. MULFORD, H. A. and MILLER, D. E. [sociologists] Drinking behavior related to definitions of alcohol; a report of research in progress. Amer. sociol. Rev. 24: 385–389, 1959.

143. MULFORD, H. A. and MILLER, D. E. Drinking in Iowa. I. Sociocultural distribution of drinkers; with a methodological model for sampling evaluation and interpretation of findings. Quart. J. Stud. Alc. 20: 704–726, 1959.

144. MULFORD, H. A. and MILLER, D. E. Drinking in Iowa. II. The extent of drinking and selected sociocultural categories. Quart. J. Stud. Alc. 21: 26–39, 1960.

145. MULFORD, H. A. and MILLER, D. E. Drinking in Iowa. III. A scale of definitions of alcohol related to drinking behavior. Quart. J. Stud. Alc. 21: 267–278, 1960.

146. MULFORD, H. A. and MILLER, D. E. Drinking in Iowa. IV. Preoccupation with alcohol and definitions of alcohol, heavy drinking and trouble due to drinking. Quart. J. Stud. Alc. 21: 279–291, 1960.

147. MULFORD, H. A. and MILLER, D. E. Drinking in Iowa. V. Drinking and alcoholic drinking. Quart. J. Stud. Alc. 21: 483–499, 1960.

148. MULFORD, H. A. and MILLER, D. E. Preoccupation with alcohol and definitions of alcohol; a replication study of two cumulative scales. Quart. J. Stud. Alc. 24: 682–696, 1963.

149. MULFORD, H. A. and WILSON, R. W. Identifying problem drinkers in a household health survey; a description of field procedures and analytical techniques developed to measure the prevalence of alcoholism. (U.S. National Center for Health Statistics, Ser. 2, No. 16.) Washington, DC; U.S. Govt Print. Off.; 1966.

150. MURDOCK, G. P. [anthropologist] Ethnographic bibliography of North America. 3d ed. New York; Taplinger; 1960.

151. NORTHERN SCIENCE RESEARCH GROUP. List of reports by Northern Science Research Group. Ottawa; Department of Indian Affairs and Northern Development; 1971.

152. OFFICER, J. [anthropologist] The concern of the Bureau of Indian Affairs over Indian alcoholism. In: Utah School of Alcohol Studies, 1963 (202). [North American Indians and an anonymous Indian community]

153. PATTISON, E. M. [psychiatrist] A critique of alcoholism treatment concepts; with special reference to abstinence. Quart. J. Stud. Alc. 27: 49–71, 1966.

154. PATTISON, E. M. A critique of abstinence criteria in the treatment of alcoholism. Int. J. social Psychiat. 14: 268–276, 1968.

155. PATTISON, E. M., HEADLEY, E. B., GLESER, G. C. and GOTTSCHALK, L. A. [2 psychiatrists, 1 M.D., 1 psychologist] Abstinence and normal drinking; an assessment of changes in drinking patterns in alcoholics after treatment. Quart. J. Stud. Alc. 29: 610–633, 1968.

156. PITTMAN, D. J. and SNYDER, C. R., eds. [sociologists] Society, culture, and drinking patterns. New York; Wiley; 1962.

157. PLAUT, T. F. A. [sociologist] Alcoholism and public welfare. Pp. 29–42.

In: Social welfare and alcoholism; conference proceedings. Washington, DC; U.S. Dept. of Health, Education, and Welfare; 1968.

158. POPHAM, R. E. [anthropologist] The Jellinek alcoholism estimation formula and its application to Canadian data. Quart. J. Stud. Alc. 17: 559-593, 1956.

159. POPHAM, R. E. and YAWNEY, C. D., comps. [anthropologist and bibliographer] Culture and alcohol use; a bibliography of anthropological studies. 2d ed. (Addiction Research Foundation Bibliographic Series, No. 1.) Toronto; 1967.

160. REICHENBACH, D. D. [M.D.] Autopsy incidence of diseases among Southwestern American Indians. Arch. Path. 84: 81-86, 1967. [mostly Pima, Apache, Papago]

161. REIFEL, B. [Congressman, political scientist, Sioux tribal member, former Bureau of Indian Affairs reservation superintendent] Factors unique to Indian reservations that contribute to Indian drinking. In: Utah School of Alcohol Studies, 1963 (202). [North American Indians]

162. ROBBINS, R. H. [anthropologist] Drinking behavior and identity resolution. Ph.D. dissertation, University of North Carolina; 1970.

163. ROBINS, L. N., BATES, W. M. and O'NEAL, P. [sociologists] Adult drinking patterns of former problem children. Pp. 395-412. In: PITTMAN, D. J. and SNYDER, C. R., eds. Society, culture, and drinking patterns. New York; Wiley; 1962.

164. ROBINSON, D. [sociologist] The alcohologist's addiction; some implications of having lost control over the disease concept of alcoholism. Quart. J. Stud. Alc. 33: 1028-1042, 1972.

165. ROHNER, R. P. and ROHNER, E. [anthropologists] Kwakiutl: Indians of British Columbia. New York; Holt, Rinehart & Winston; 1970.

166. ROSENHAN, D. L. [psychologist] On being sane in insane places. Science 179: 250-258, 1973.

167. SALONE, E. [historian] Les sauvages du Canada et les maladies importées de France au XVIIe et au XVIIIe siècle; la picote et l'alcoolisme. J. Soc. Américanistes, Paris 4: 7-20, 1904.

168. SANCHEZ, P. R. [guidance specialist, B.I.A.] Nature of the alcoholism problem. (3 pp.) In: Utah School of Alcohol Studies, 1967 (202). [North American Indians]

169. SAVARD, R. J. [social worker] Effects of disulfiram therapy on relationships within the Navaho drinking group. Quart. J. Stud. Alc. 29: 909-916, 1968.

170. SCHOOLCRAFT, H. R. [ethnologist] Inquiries respecting the history, present condition and future prospects of the Indian tribes of the United States. Washington, DC; U.S. Govt Print. Off.; 1847.

171. SEELEY, J. R. [sociologist] Estimating the prevalence of alcoholism; a critical analysis of the Jellinek formula. Quart. J. Stud. Alc. 20: 245-254, 1959.

172. SEELEY, J. R. The W.H.O. definition of alcoholism. Quart. J. Stud. Alc. 20: 352-356, 1959.

173. SIEGLER, M., OSMOND, H. and NEWELL, S. [sociologist, psychiatrist, ?] Models of alcoholism. Quart. J. Stud. Alc. 29: 571-591, 1968.

174. Sievers, M. L. [M.D.] Cigarette and alcohol usage by southwestern American Indians. Amer. J. publ. Hlth 58: 71–82, 1968.

175. Slotkin, J. S. [anthropologist] Social psychiatry of Menomini community. J. abnorm. social Psychol. 48: 10–16, 1953.

176. Smith, J. A. [psychiatrist] Psychiatric research in the etiology of alcoholism. Pp. 5–15. In: Pittman, D. J., ed. Alcoholism; an interdisciplinary approach. Springfield, IL; Thomas; 1959.

177. Snyder, C. R. [sociologist] Alcohol and the Jews; a cultural study of drinking and sobriety. (Rutgers Center of Alcohol Studies, Monogr. No. 1.) New Brunswick, NJ; 1958.

178. Snyder, P. Z. [anthropologist] Social assimilation and adjustment of Navajo migrants to Denver, Colorado. (Navajo urban relocation research project. Rep. No. 13.) Boulder; University of Colorado Institute of Behavioral Science; 1968.

179. Southwest Indian Alcoholism Council. Annual report. Scottsdale, AZ; 1965.

180. Spang, A. T., Sr. [assistant director, Technical Assistance, CAP, Arizona State University] Community action program alcoholism components. In: Annual report. Scottsdale, AZ; Southwest Indian Alcoholism Council; 1965. [Jicarilla Apache]

181. Spindler, G. D. and Spindler, L. S. [anthropologists] American Indian personality types and their sociocultural roots. Ann. Amer. Acad. polit. social Sci. 311: 147–157, 1957. [North American Indians]

182. Spradley, J. P. [anthropologist] You owe yourself a drunk; an ethnography of urban nomads. Boston; Little, Brown; 1970.

183. Steiner, C. [psychologist] Games alcoholics play; the analysis of life scripts. New York; Grove; 1971.

184. Stewart, O. C. [anthropologist] Questions regarding American Indian criminality. Hum. Organiz. 23: 61–66, 1964. [North American Indians]

185. Suarez, E. [Chief, Division of Law and Order, B.I.A.] Testimony of Eugene Suarez. In: Hearings Before a Subcommittee on Department of the Interior and Related Agencies of the Committee on Appropriations, House of Representatives, 92nd Congress, 1st session. Pt. 1. Washington, DC; 1971.

186. Syme, L. [sociologist] Personality characteristics and the alcoholic; a critique of current studies. Quart. J. Stud. Alc. 18: 288–302, 1957.

187. Szuter, C. F., Savard, R. J. and Saiki, J. H. [2 M.D.s, 1 social worker] The use of disulfiram in treatment of alcoholic problems in an American Indian population. Fort Defiance, AZ; U.S. Public Health Service, Fort Defiance Indian Hospital; 1965.

188. Thurber, J. The bear who let it alone. [Orig. 1931.] In: The Thurber carnival. New York; Random House; 1957.

189. Tiebout, H. M., Williams, L., Selzer, M. L., Block, M. A., Fox, R., Zwerling, I., Armstrong, J. D., Esser, P. H., Bell, R. G., Smith, J. A., Thimann, J., Myerson, D. J., Lolli, G., Davies, D. L., Lemere, F., Kjølstad, T., Brunner-Orne, M. and Maidman, M. M. Normal drinking in recovered alcoholics; comments on the article by D. L. Davies. Quart. J. Stud. Alc. 24: 109–121, 321–332, 727–735, 1963.

190. THWAITES, R. G., ed. [historian] Jesuit relations and allied documents, 1601–1791. 74 vol. Cleveland; Burrows Brothers; 1896–1901. [Indians of New France]

191. TOLER, F. M. [director, New Mexico Commission on Alcoholism] Developing a state program for Indian alcohol problems. In: Utah School of Alcohol Studies, 1966 (202). [Indians of New Mexico]

192. TRICE, H. M. [sociologist] A study of the process of affiliation with Alcoholics Anonymous. Ph.D. dissertation, University of Wisconsin; 1957.

193. TRICE, H. M. The affiliation motive and readiness to join Alcoholics Anonymous. Quart. J. Stud. Alc. 20: 313–320, 1959.

194. TRICE, H. M. and WAHL, J. R. A rank order analysis of the symptoms of alcoholism. Quart. J. Stud. Alc. 19: 636–648, 1958.

195. TRILLIN, C. [journalist] U.S. Journal: Gallup, New Mexico; drunken Indians. The New Yorker, 25 September 1971.

196. ULLMAN, A. D. [sociologist] Sociocultural backgrounds of alcoholism. Ann. Amer. Acad. polit. social Sci. 351: 48–54, 1958.

197. ULLMAN, A. D. To know the difference. New York; St. Martin's; 1960.

198. U.S. DEPARTMENT OF HEALTH, EDUCATION, AND WELFARE, PUBLIC HEALTH SERVICE, BUREAU OF MEDICAL SERVICES, DIVISION OF INDIAN HEALTH. Indian health highlights. Washington, DC; U.S. Govt Print. Off.; 1966. [North American Indians]

199. U.S. NATIONAL CENTER FOR PREVENTION AND CONTROL OF ALCOHOLISM. Alcohol and alcoholism. (Public Health Service Publ. No. 1640.) Washington, DC; U.S. Govt Print. Off.; 1967.

200. USHIJIMA, M. Nushidori and ko in Suye Mura; social role in the process of change. Jap. sociol. Rev. 13: 64–86, 1962.

201. UTAH SCHOOL OF ALCOHOL STUDIES. Bibliography of American Indian drinking and alcoholism literature. Salt Lake City; University of Utah; 1967. [mimeographed]

202. UTAH SCHOOL OF ALCOHOL STUDIES. Lectures and reports; manual supplement. Salt Lake City; University of Utah; 1963–1967.

203. VACHON, A. [historian] L'eau-de-vie dans la société Indienne. Pp. 22–23. In: Annual report. Canadian Historical Association; 1960. [Indians of New France]

204. VAN VALKENBURGH, R. [anthropologist] Navajo common law. II. Navajo law and justice. Mus. Notes, Mus. nth. Ariz. 9: 51–54, 1937.

205. WALLACE, S. E. [sociologist] Skid Row as a way of life. Totowa, NJ; Bedminster Press; 1965.

206. WALLGREN, H. and BARRY, H., 3d [zoophysiologist and psychologist] Actions of alcohol. Vol. I. Biochemical, physiological and psychological aspects. Vol. II. Chronic and clinical aspects. New York; Elsevier; 1970.

207. WANG, R. P. [M.D.] A study of alcoholism in Chinatown. Int. J. social Psychiat. 14: 260–267, 1968.

208. WASHBURNE, C. [anthropologist] Primitive drinking; a study of the uses and functions of alcohol in preliterate societies. New Haven; College & University Press; 1961. [Papago, pp. 172–184]

209. WERNER, V. W. [executive director, Southwest Indian Alcoholism Council] New Mexico state alcoholism program. In: Utah School of Alcohol Studies, 1963 (202). [Indians of New Mexico]

210. WESTERN REGION INDIAN ALCOHOLISM TRAINING CENTER. Indian tribes funded for alcoholism programs by O.E.O., 1970–71. Salt Lake City; Bureau of Indian Services, University of Utah; 1971.

211. WHITE, R. [sociologist] The urbanization of the Dakota Indians. M.A. thesis, St. Louis University; 1960.

212. WHITTAKER, J. O. [psychologist] Alcohol and the Standing Rock Sioux tribe. I. The pattern of drinking. Quart. J. Stud. Alc. 23: 468–479, 1962.

213. WHITTAKER, J. O. Alcohol and the Standing Rock Sioux tribe. II. Psychodynamic and cultural factors in drinking. Quart. J. Stud. Alc. 24: 80–90, 1963.

214. WILKINS, W. L. and WESSON, A. F. [psychologist and sociologist] Studying the social epidemiology of alcoholism. Pp. 72–77. In: PITTMAN, D. J., ed. Alcoholism; an interdisciplinary approach. Springfield, IL; Thomas; 1959.

215. WILKINSON, R. L. [political scientist] The prevention of drinking problems; alcohol control and cultural influences. New York; Oxford; 1970.

216. WINKLER, A. M. [historian] Drinking on the American frontier. Quart. J. Stud. Alc. 29: 413–445, 1968.

217. WISSLER, C. [anthropologist] Indians of the United States; four centuries of their history and culture. Garden City; Doubleday; 1940. Cit. Indian Health Service Task Force (76).

218. WORLD HEALTH ORGANIZATION, EXPERT COMMITTEE ON ALCOHOL AND ALCOHOLISM. Alcohol and alcoholism; report of an expert committee. (WHO Tech. Rep. Ser., No. 94.) Geneva; 1955.

219. WORLD HEALTH ORGANIZATION, EXPERT COMMITTEE ON MENTAL HEALTH. First report of the Alcoholism Subcommittee. (WHO Tech. Rep. Ser., No. 42.) Geneva; 1951.

220. WORLD HEALTH ORGANIZATION, EXPERT COMMITTEE ON MENTAL HEALTH. Second report of the Alcoholism Subcommittee. (WHO Tech. Rep. Ser., No. 48.) Geneva; 1952.

221. YOUNG, R. W. The Navaho yearbook, Vol. 8. Window Rock, AZ, Navaho Agency; 1961.

222. American Indian workshop sessions. In: Utah School of Alcohol Studies, 1964 (202). [North American Indians]

223. 'I believe in Apartheid,' says spokeswoman [Kahn-Tineta Horn, Iroquois]. Akwesasne Notes, Wesleyan Univ., Middleton, CT 3 (No. 5): 41, 1971. ["Indians"]

224. Indian workshop report: Colville. In: Utah School of Alcohol Studies, 1963 (202).

225. The liquor problem among Indians of the Southwest. Indian Affairs, NY 18: 3–4, 1956. [Navaho]

Unpublished Documents

226. ANDRE, J. M. [M.D.] A psychiatrist looks at general problems in Indian communities. (11 pp.) Presented at the 6th Annual Institute on Alcohol Studies, sponsored by the New Mexico Commission on Alcoholism and Western New Mexico University, Silver City, NM, 24 June 1970. [Indians of New Mexico]

227. BOLLINGER, H. E. and STARKEY, V. L. Survey of problems on a southwestern Indian reservation. Unpublished USPHS report, Mescalero, NM, June 1966. Cit. Littman (116, 117). [Mescalero Apache]

228. CLASSIFIED ABSTRACT ARCHIVE OF THE ALCOHOL LITERATURE. Bibliography on "American Indians and alcohol." New Brunswick, NJ; Rutgers Center of Alcohol Studies; 1969.

229. EVERETT, M. W. [anthropologist] White Mountain Apache inter-generational problem drinking. Presented at the Annual Meeting of the American Anthropological Association, Toronto, 1 November 1972.

230. GEERTZ, C. [anthropologist] Drought, death and alcohol in five southwestern cultures. Unpublished manuscript, Harvard University Values Study; 1951. [Zuni, Navaho]

231. HONIGMANN, J. J. [anthropologist] Adaptation of Indians, Eskimo and persons of partial indigenous background in a Canadian Northern town. Presented at the 67th annual meeting of the American Anthropological Association, Seattle, 1968.

232. HONIGMANN, J. J. Formation of Mackenzie Delta frontier culture. (9 pp.) Presented at the Northeastern Anthropological Society, Ottawa, 7–9 May 1970. [Eskimo, Indians and other natives of Inuvik]

233. HONIGMANN, J. J. and HONIGMANN, I. Alcohol in a Canadian Northern town. Working paper No. 1, Urbanization in the Arctic and Subarctic. (81 pp.) Presented at the meeting of the Canadian Sociology and Anthropology Association, 1968. [anonymous Canadian town]

234. HONIGMANN, J. J. and HONIGMANN, I. Success in school; adaptation in a new Canadian Arctic town. (85 pp.) 1969. [Eskimo, Indians and other natives of Inuvik]

235. KAPLAN, B. [anthropologist] The social functions of Navaho "heavy drinking." Presented at the Annual Meeting of the Society for Applied Anthropology, Kansas City, 1962. Cit. Whittaker (213).

236. KILEN, A. A. [alcoholism project employee] Alcoholism program evaluation. (48 pp.) Reno; Inter-Tribal Council of Nevada; 1969. [Washo, Paiute and Shoshone of Nevada]

237. MINDELL, C. [M.D.] Clinical aspects of the use of alcohol among the Oglala Sioux. Presented at the Rosebud Sioux Tribe workshop on alcohol, Rosebud, SD, 10–11 October 1967.

238. SLATER, A. D. [professor of personnel and guidance] A study of the extent and costs of excessive drinking on the Uintah-Ouray Indian reservation. (31 pp.) Unpublished ms. Provo, UT; Dept. of Personnel and Guidance, Brigham Young University; 1967. [Subsequently published in BAHR, H. M. et al., eds. Native Americans today. New York; Harper & Row; 1972.]

239. SLATER, A. D. Study of attitudes towards the use of alcoholic beverages found among the Ute Indians. (26 pp.) Unpublished ms. Provo, UT; Brigham Young University; 1967.

240. SOBELL, M. B. and SOBELL, L. C. The need for realism, relevance and operational assumptions in the study of substance abuse. Presented at the International Symposia on Alcohol and Drug Research, Addiction Research Foundation, Toronto, 1973. (To be published as proceedings, No. 6.)

241. SWETT, D. H. [anthropologist] Characteristics of the male Indian arrest population in San Francisco. Prepared for a symposium on urban adjustment of American Indians, Southwest Anthropological Association Conference. University of California, Riverside, 1963. [Indians in San Francisco from various tribes]

Index of Subjects

155